Essence of World Religions

Unity in Diversity

Compiled by

Pravin K. Shah

Chairperson / JAINA Education Committee
Federation of Jain Associations in North America

Director / Jain Study Center of North Carolina

509 Carriage Woods Circle, Raleigh NC 27607

Essence of World Religions
First Edition: July 1994
Second Edition (revised): April 2004

ISBN: 1-59406-040-1

This book has no copyright

Distributed by:

JAINA Education Committee - Federation of Jain Associations in North America

Jain Study Center of North Carolina (Raleigh)

509 Carriage Woods Circle
Raleigh, NC 27607-3969 USA

Email - education@jaina.org
Telephone and Fax - 919-859-4994
Website – www.jaina.org

We are interested in your comments.
Please use the above address for communication.

PREFACE

Has religion ever confused and confounded you? If so, this booklet is compiled just for you. It is our humble attempt to bring together a simple summary of the world's major spiritual paths.

The primary source of this book is an article, an insert in the Hinduism Today newspaper of April 1993, and its earlier version. The article has been expanded by using several other sources and reviewing it with many people of different faiths. The most of material of the introduction chapter is taken from the Parliament of world religion book.

The strength of this book is its simplicity. However this causes other problems such as the complex and subtle distinctions and certain important exceptions of various religions are consciously set aside for the sake of simplicity. There are hundreds of books addressing deeper matters, but few of them have attempted a straightforward, comparative summary.

By comparing a few major beliefs of the great religions, we hope to highlight how their paths are similar and how they differ. Unless you are already a comparative religion expert, a leisurely hour with this book will endow you with a good grasp of the essential truths of every major faith practiced today.

The following basic information of each religion is compiled in this book:

- Founded   - Founder   - Major Scriptures

- Sects   - Adherents   - Synopses

- Beliefs- Symbols   - Holidays

At the end, there is a comparison between Indian and Western religions.

The first edition of this book was compiled for the first generation of Young Jains of North America (YJA) for their first national convention in 1994. YJA is a dedicated group of youth who are very sincere in establishing the proper roots of Jain ethics, principles, and religion. However it is extremely important to understand the basic philosophy and values of all major world religions in order to understand Jain principles and ethics properly. With this idea in mind the first edition of this booklet was compiled. In this second edition, we have added/ modified certain information on each religion based on the feedback we have received.

By profession I am an Electrical Engineer, Jain by faith, and I teach Jainism and comparative religions to Jain youth and adults of North America during my spare time. Hence there is a possibility that I may not have compiled the description of other religions properly. Please pardon us for any mistake, oversight, understatement, or overstatement in the material. We request you to use the material objectively and provide positive suggestions so that we can incorporate them easily in future revisions.

I am very thankful to Sudhir and Anita Shah of Connecticut for their help in the print layout, formatting, cover design, and other valuable suggestions. Without their help I could not have published it before the Parliament of World Religions Conference of July 2004. I am thankful to my daughter Shweta Shah, a close friend Samuel E. Wallace, Rekha Banker, Shanti Mohnot, and many others who edited various aspects of the book. Sam also provided valuable suggestions on the Western religions. I am also thankful to Helen Park of Oriental Art Press for printing this book on a priority basis.

Thank You.

Pravin K. Shah   April 10, 2004

"Believe nothing, no matter where you read it, or who said it - even if I have said it - unless it agrees with your own reason and your own common sense."

- The Buddha

"Do all the good you can, By all the means you can, In all the ways you can, In all the places you can, At all the times you can, To all the people you can, As long as ever you can."

- John Wesley

Contents

DEDICATED

TO

People Around the World
Committed to Compassionate Living

for their continued effort in promoting Non-violence, protection of the environment and a spirit of compassionate interdependence with nature and all living beings.

Special thanks to the people practicing a Vegan and Alcohol/drug free life-style for inspiring us to see a true connection between the principle of Non-violence and the choices we make.

A vegan and alcohol/drug free life-style stems from a compelling set of ethical and moral value system, where one makes a conscious effort to minimize harm to all animals and to our own body, mind & soul. As a result, one avoids the use of all animal products such as meat, fish, chicken, eggs, milk, cheese, ice-cream, and all dairy products as well as silk, fur, pearls and leather. One also refrains from all types of addictive substances such as alcohol and drugs.

Introduction

During the thousands of years, search of mankind's history and man's search for God or Self has led down many pathways. The result has been the enormous diversity of religious expression found worldwide. It ranges from the endless variety of Hinduism; the emptiness of Buddhism; the self-control of Jainism; and the harmonious approach of Sikhism; to the monotheism of Judaism, Christianity, and Islam; and to the oriental philosophies of Shinto, Taoism, and Confucianism.

The prophets of all religions have realized the same whole reality / truth, but only their language differs. All preach reverence for truth, honesty, dignity, freedom, and human brotherhood, and yet when we look at the history of the world it appears that much blood has been shed in the name of religion.

In every religion there are three elements:

Philosophy or basic Belief

Mythology

Rituals

A close study of all scriptures reveal that the basic beliefs like faith in God or Self, reverence for truth, honesty, and brotherly love are common. The differences exist in rituals and mythology. This is due to the fact that various religions have developed in different times, places and within various cultural contexts.

In what way and how many times a day should God be worshipped?

Whether or not there should be provision for divorce?

Whether or not birth control or use of contraceptives is allowed in religion?

All these questions are important and yet whether any social custom is moral or immoral, good or bad, depends on the specific time, place and circumstances. Hence it is important that the moral code of our time must respond to the needs of modern human beings and their problems rather than observing traditions that have become obsolete.

Secondly in our scientific age, there can be no place for magic, miracles, myths, or superstitious clinging to traditional dogmas.

The basic principles never change, and that is what is important to follow and preach. The true progress of humans on earth is the progress of their vision to visualize the:

- Cosmic greatness of Hinduism
- Joy in truth of Buddha
- Spiritual victory of Jainism
- Harmony of Sikh Gurus
- Wisdom of Confucius
- Simple love of Tao
- Moral and Spiritual Uprightness of Shintoism
- One God of Israel
- Moral issues of Zoroaster
- Redeeming radiance of Christianity
- Glory of God of Islam
- Unity of Mankind and World peace of Bahä'i

In all of them we have Lamps of Fire that burn in the glory of God / Self.

Lead me from Unreality to Reality
Lead me from Darkness to Light
Lead me from Death to Immortality

- Yajur Veda (Hinduism)

"A journey of a thousand miles begins with a single step."

- Confucius

Religion does not guarantee that there shall be no sorrow or suffering. But it does guarantee that there shall be strength to face them calmly.

- Unknown

Religions of
India

BUDDHISM

परस्परोपग्रहो जीवानाम्
Compassionate Living

HINDUISM

JAINISM

SIKHISM

Hinduism

Founded

Hinduism is the world's oldest living religion. It has no beginning as it predates recorded history.

Founder

Hinduism has no human founder.

Major Scriptures

Hinduism believes that its original scriptures have no authors. The learned sages who collected this literature are mere vehicles of the Divine. The earliest collections are the four Vedäs (bodies of knowledge) which are written in verse and contain hymns, chants, prayers, poems, riddles, and legends. Other collections build upon the Vedic legacy. The 108 Upanishadas contain philosophical and mystical teachings of the ancient sages (900 BC to 200 BC). The Puränas (religious lore) are medieval collections of laws, stories, folk literature and philosophy. The Bhagavada Gitä (Song of God) is a part of the great epic Mahäbhärata. It has been called the Hindu Bible.

Sects

There are four main denominations:

- Shaivism – Follower of Lord Shiva
- Shaktism – Follower of Shakti (Female form of Supreme)
- Vaishnavism – Follower of Lord Vishnu
- Liberalism – Follower of Brahman (non sectarian forms)

Adherents

Over 800 million; mostly in India, Sri Lanka, Nepal, Malaysia, Indonesia, Mauritius, Africa, Europe and North and South America.

Goals

The ultimate goal of Hinduism is Moksha or liberation (total freedom). This is the personal and direct realization of one's true divine self, which grants permanent liberation from the cycle of rebirth, or Samsär. This realization is termed Nirvikalpa Samädhi and is the totally transcendent culmination of yoga. For monists, this means total merger in oneness and identity. For dualists it means a loving, blessed union with God in which the individuality of the soul is maintained.

Hindu philosophy is essentially a philosophy of values. Hindu sages classify the values into four groups. They are Käm (psychophysical values), Artha (economic values), Dharma (moral values), and Moksha (spiritual values). Moksha or liberation is the highest value of human life. The final destiny of all souls is union with the Supreme, most widely revered as Shiva for Shaivism, Shakti for Shaktism, Vishnu for Vaishnavism, and Brahman for Liberalism.

In the process of spiritual uplift, one conquers the state of ignorance (Avidya) which causes the illusionary world to appear as real. All illusion has vanished for realized beings (Jivanmukta).

A secondary goal for Shaivism is Savikalpa Samädhi or experience of God Shiva as Sat Chit Änand or consciousness full of truth and bliss.

A secondary goal for Shaktism is to perform good work selflessly. For Shaktas, God is both the formless Absolute (Shiva) and the manifest Divine (Shakti or Goddess Durgä Käli). However, importance is given to the feminine manifest by which the masculine unmanifest (Shiva) is ultimately reached.

A secondary goal of Vaishnavism is the experience of God's Grace, which can be reached while yet embodied through taking refuge in God's unbounded love. Lord Vishnu is God, all pervasive consciousness and the soul of the universe.

Path of Attainment

Hinduism believes that each soul is free to find his own way to liberation by following the path of devotion (Bhakti Yoga), path of knowledge (Jnän Yoga), path of yoga and meditation (Räja Yoga), or path of selfless service (Karma Yoga). It relies strongly on the studying, listening, and recitation of the Vedäs, Ägams, Gitä, Upanishadas, Puräna, and other sacred scriptures. It values devotion, yoga, and contemplative spiritual practice (Sädhanä).

The path for Shaivism divides the spiritual progress of the soul into four progressive stages of belief and practice, called Charya, Kriyä, Yoga, and Jnän. The soul evolves through the process of reincarnation, gradually maturing from the instinctive intellectual sphere into virtuous and moral living. It then progresses into temple worship and devotion, followed by yoga, meditation. The sustained and consistent practice of yoga brings union with God through the grace of the living true teacher (Sat Guru) and culminates in the soul's maturity, the state of wisdom (Jnän).

The spiritual practices in Shaktism are similar to those in Shaivism. There is more emphasis on Shakti, God's power as opposed to being, and on embracing apparent opposites: male and female, absolute and relative, pleasure and pain, cause and effect, mind and body. A minor sect undertakes Tantric practices, consciously using the world of form to transmute and eventually transcend that world.

Orthodox Vaishnavites believe that religion is the performance of devotion (Bhakti Sädhanä) with which man can communicate with and receive the grace of Lord Vishnu who manifests through the temple deity or idol. All other paths, the path of selfless service (Karma Yoga), path of knowledge (Jnän Yoga), and path of yoga and meditation (Räja Yoga) lead to devotion (Bhakti Yoga). By chanting the holy names of Lord Vishnu's incarnations (Lord Räma or Lord Krishna) and total self surrender to Him, liberation is attained.

Most Liberal Hindus believe that Mukti or Liberation is achieved through Jnän yoga alone which is defined as intellectual and meditative. Devotees may also choose from three other paths to acquire good karma, cultivate devotion, and purify the mind. This non-sectarian sect follows the Advaita Vedänta philosophy of Ädi Shankara. Their worship includes a wide range of deities.

Beliefs

One Supreme Being who is all pervasive and who is both imminent and transcendent, both ever-present and beyond time and space – simultaneously a Creator (Lord Brahmä), a Sustainer (Lord Vishnu), and a Destroyer (Lord Shiva).

The universe undergoes endless cycles of creation, preservation, and dissolution.

The various deities represent many aspects, powers, and functions of the one divine Ultimate Reality or Supreme Being.

All souls are evolving towards a union with God and will ultimately attain spiritual knowledge and liberation from the cycle of rebirth. Not a single soul will be eternally deprived of this destiny.

Karma is the law of cause and effect by which each individual creates his own destiny by his thoughts, words, and deeds.

The soul reincarnates, evolving through many births until all karma has been resolved.

Divine beings exist in unseen inner worlds and temple worship rituals and sacraments, as well as personal devotions, creating a communion with the gods (Devas) and Gods.

To know the transcendent absolute, a spiritually awakened master (Sat Guru) is essential as are individual discipline, good conduct, purification, self-inquiry, and meditation.

In the practice of Non-violence (Ahimsä) all life is sacred and to be loved and revered.

All genuine religious paths are facets of God's pure love and light, deserving tolerance and understanding and are acceptable means to the divine.

Synopsis

Hinduism is a vast and profound religion. It worships one supreme Reality (called by many names) and teaches that all souls ultimately realize truth. There is no eternal hell or damnation. It accepts all genuine spiritual paths, from pure monism (God alone exists) to theistic dualism (when shall I know His Grace?). Each soul is free to find his/her own way, whether by devotion, knowledge, austerity, meditation, yoga, or selfless service. Hinduism believes in the philosophy of karma, rebirth, and the immortality of Soul. It also believes that God is a creator of the universe but the creation and creator are not different. In other words God is the universe and the universe is God. Hence there is no beginning or end of the universe.

In its diversity, Hinduism hardly fits most Western definitions of religion; rather, it suggests commitment to or respect for an ideal way of life, known as Dharma.

Historically Hinduism has developed over about 4,000 years and has no single founder or creed. Rather, it consists of a vast variety of beliefs and practices. Organization is minimal and hierarchy is non-existent.

Temple worship, scripture, and master (Guru) and disciple (Shishya) tradition are emphasized. Festivals, pilgrimages, chanting of holy hymns and home worship are dynamic practices. Hinduism explains that the soul reincarnates until all karma are resolved and the realization of God is attained.

The magnificent holy temples, the peaceful piety of the Hindu homes, the subtle metaphysics, and the science of yoga all play their part. Love, Non-violence, good conduct, and the law of Dharma define the Hindu path. Hinduism is a mystical religion, leading the truth within, finally reaching the pinnacle of consciousness where man and God are one.

Caste System

The ancient texts suggest four great classes, or castes to stabilize and strengthen the society. The origin of the caste was not birth but ability to efficiently perform certain specific duties.

- Brahmins or priests:

  To establish and preserve national ideas and philosophy
- Kshatriyas or warriors and rulers:

  To protect the state from aggression and to establish internal order
- Vaisyas or merchants:

  To aid in the production of national wealth
- Shudras or farmers and laborers:

  To do the labor work

Some of the Shudras are classified as Untouchables, which includes those occupations that require them to handle unclean objects. Besides the duties that are derived from an individual's caste, general duties are also incumbent on all moral beings.

These include honesty, courage, service, faith, self-control, purity, and Non-violence.

Stages of Life

The classical works also outline four ideal stages (Äshrams) of life, each with its own duties:

- Student (Brahmacharya):
  from initiation (childhood) until marriage
- Householders (Gruhastha):
  raise family, provide support, and help in the uplift of the society
- Forest dwelling (Vanaprasthya):
  transfer household duties to grown children and retire and dedicate your life to social and charity work
- Renunciation (Sanyäsa):
  give up attachment to all worldly things and seek spiritual liberation

These ideal castes and stages encompass males only. The position of women in Hinduism has always been ambiguous. On one hand they are venerated as a symbol of the divine; on the other, they are treated as inferior beings. Women were traditionally expected to serve their husbands and they should not have any independent interests. Recent movements within Hinduism, such as the Brahma Samäj, have succeeded in altering this situation.

Hindu Deities

Hindus believe that the universe is populated by a multitude of gods. To some extent, these gods share the features of Godhood but are seen as behaving much as humans do and as being related to each other as humans are. This view is similar to that of the ancient Greeks. The sets of gods recognized by the different sects are not mutually exclusive.

The supreme Gods Brahmä, Vishnu, and Shiva, and Vishnu's incarnations such as Räma and Krishna are often viewed as activated through their relationships with female deities. These female consorts of the deities are called Shakti.

Some other well known gods are said to be related to other gods, such as Ganesha, the elephant headed god, is a son of Lord Shiva and Pärvati. Hanumän, the monkey-faced god, is a faithful disciple of Lord Räma. Käli or Durgä is Lord Shiva's consort.

Symbols

The Sanskrit OM symbolizes God in Hinduism. God is one. However sages call Him by various names. Though these names differ from one another, all of them have sprung up from the same basic source of all sounds called Om. Hence, OM represents all names of God.

OM comprises of three independent letters a, u, and m. Each letter has its own meaning and significance. The letter "a" represents beginning (ädimatva), "u" represents progress (utkarsha), and "m" represents limit or dissolution (miti). The word OM represents the power responsible for creation, development, and dissolution of this universe, which is God Himself.

Holidays

The over 2000-year-old Hindu calendar is lunar, adjusted to the solar seasons. The new and full-moon days and the eleventh day of each month are believed to be auspicious.

There are at least as many Hindu holidays as there are deities - at least one for every day of the year! They are observed by pujä, prayer, feasts, fasts, dance, chants, and readings of sacred texts.

- Janmäshtami - Lord Krishna's birthday
- Ganesha Chaturthi - Birthday of the elephant-headed God of Success
- Navarätri - Ten day festival of goddesses marks the prayer of Durgä, Ambä, Bahuchar etc..)
- Diwäli - Festival of Lights marks Lord Vishnu's triumph over evil and honors goddess Lakshmi (goddess of wealth and prosperity) and in some regions goddess Käli.
- Holi - Honors young Lord Krishna's triumph over evil Holikä.
- Shivarätri - Lord Shiva's birthday

Buddhism

Founded

2,500 year ago in India

Founder

Gautama Siddhärtha known as Buddha, who was the most recent in a long series of Buddhas.

Major Scriptures

"Tripitaka" (three baskets of wisdom) is for the Therävada sect. It is written in the Päli Präkrit language. It contains discourses (Sutta), rules of conduct (Vinaya), and analysis of doctrine (Abhidhamma).

"Sutras" is for Mahäyäna sects. The major Sutras are Anguttara Nikaya, Dhammapada, Sutta Nipatta, and Samyutta Nikaya. They are written in Sanskrit overlapped with Päli.

Sects

There are two main sects, Therävada (Hinayäna) and Mahäyäna. The Therävada, or "Way of the Elders," is the more conservative of the two. It is dominant in Sri Lanka, Burma, and Thailand.

The Mahäyäna, or "Great Vehicle," is more diverse and liberal. It is mainly found in Taiwan, Korea, and Japan, and among Tibetan peoples, where it is distinguished by its emphasis on the Buddhist Tantras. Zen Buddhism is a major sect of Mahäyäna.

Adherents

Over 300 million in China, Japan, Sri Lanka, Thailand, Myanmar (Burma), Indonesia, Korea, and Tibet.

Goals

The primary goal of Buddhism is Nirvana, defined as the end of change, and literally meaning "to blow out" as one blows out a candle. The Therävada tradition describes the indescribable as peace and tranquility. The Mahäyäna tradition views it as emptiness and the unchanging essence of the Buddha and ultimate reality.

Nirvana is synonymous with release from the bonds of desire, ego, suffering, and rebirth. Buddha never defined the term except to say, "It is unborn, unoriginated, unmade, and uncompounded". Nirvana is not a state of annihilation, but of peace and reality. Buddhism does not believe in a creator God and thus no union with God.

Path of Attainment

Buddhism takes its followers through progressive stages of spiritual progress, namely Dhyäna, Samapatti, and Samädhi.

- Dhyäna is meditation, which leads to moral and intellectual purification, and to detachment, which leads to pure consciousness.

- Samapatti, or further Dhyäna, leads to a state that is perfect solitude. This leads further to Samädhi.

- Samädhi is the attainment of supernatural consciousness and finally to Nirvana.

Synopsis

The goal of life is Nirvana. Buddha's essential teachings contain the four Noble Truths:

- Suffering:

  Life is permeated by suffering or dissatisfaction. Being born, old age, sickness, and death are all suffering. Union with what we dislike is suffering; separation from what we desire is suffering. This is the essential nature of life.

- Cause of Suffering:

  Desire or craving is the cause of suffering. It is the force of desire that leads to rebirth and further suffering, accompanied by delight and passion.

- Cessation of Suffering:

The complete cessation of desires or cravings will end the suffering. Forsaking, relinquishing, and detaching of ourselves from desire and craving will automatically end the pain, pleasure, birth and rebirth.

- The Path to end the Suffering:

  By practicing the noble eight fold path, one can end the suffering:

  Right belief

  Right thought or aim

  Right speech

  Right action

  Right livelihood or occupation

  Right effort or endeavor

  Right mindfulness

  Right meditation

The first two concern the preliminary frame of mind of the aspirant; the next three are the ethical requirements; the last three concern meditative training needed to realize ultimate truth and peace. This attainment of peace is called Nirvana.

Beliefs

The Supreme is completely transcendent and can be described as Sunya, a void, an emptiness, or state of non being.

The Four Noble Truths are:

- Suffering exists
- Desire is the cause of Suffering
- Cessation of Desire or Thrust ends Suffering
- To end Desire one must follow the Eight Fold path

Life's aim is to end suffering through the annihilation of individual ego, desire, or thrust and hence its existence and absorption into Nirvana.

Individuals have three characteristics – suffering (Dukkha), absence of an eternal self (Anattä), and impermanence (Aniccä).

Man's true nature is divine and eternal, yet his individuality is subject to change that affect all forms and is therefore transient, dissolving at liberation into Nirvana. The no-self doctrine implies that living beings have no eternal souls.

In the sanctity of the Buddha and in the sacred scriptures of Buddhism; the Tripitaka (three Baskets of Wisdom) and the Mahäyäna Sutras.

The greatness of self giving love and compassion towards all creatures that contain merit exceeding the giving of offering to the gods.

Dharma (the path), Karma (cause and effect), Reincarnation, Sangh (unity of seekers), and the passage on earth as an opportunity to end the cycle of birth and death.

The Middle Path consists of living moderately and avoiding extremes of luxury and asceticism.

The monastic life is necessary to attain Nirvana.

The duties of an individual are defined in the Five precepts (Panchashila) – Non-violence (also towards all animals), Non-stealing, Truthfulness (speak only harmless truth otherwise observe silence), Immoral sensual relationship, and Avoidance of Drugs and Alcohol.

Symbols

- Wheel:

  The Dharma Chakra or the Wheel of the Law is the most important symbol of Buddhism. The wheel signifies the circle of births and deaths due to karma, which a person personally keeps in motion through his thirst (Tanhä) for life. It also symbolizes a constantly changing universe, and the impermanence of everything in the world. The hub of the wheel represents the three causes of pain: illwill, ignorance, and lust.

  The eight spokes of the wheel represent the eightfold path. The wheel cannot survive without the spokes. Even so, Dharma cannot be sustained without the practice of these eight virtues.

Holidays

Buddhist holidays celebrate important moments of the life of the Buddha such as His birth, Enlightenment, and entry into Nirvana;

his teachings; and aspects of the interaction of monks and laypeople. It is marked with home decorations, pageantry, processions, and the devotional practices. Buddhist holiday dates vary widely from one Asian country to another, and from one tradition to another.

- American Zen Buddhists celebrate the Buddha's birthday as Buddha Day in May.
- Hana - Matsuri (April 8) is a Japanese celebration of the Buddha's Enlightenment.
- The birthday of Rinzai Zenji, the founder of the Rinzai school of Zen Buddhism is celebrated on January 10. Zen Buddhist holidays involve sitting meditation (zazen), chanting, singing, drumming, and socializing.

The Formula

The mystic was back from the desert. "Tell us," people said, "what God is like."

But how could he ever tell them what he had experienced in his heart? Can God be put into words?

He finally gave them a formula – inaccurate, inadequate – in the hope that some might be tempted to experience it for themselves.

They seized upon the formula. They made it sacred text. They imposed it on others as a holy belief. They went to great pains to spread it in foreign lands. Some even gave their lives for it.

The mystic was sad. It might have been better if he had said nothing.

The Zen Master says: "The one who knows does not say. The one who says does not know."

Jainism

परस्परोपग्रहो जीवानाम्
Compassionate Living

परस्परोपग्रहो जीवानाम्
Compassionate Living

Founded

Jainism is one of the oldest living religions. It has no beginning. It predates recorded history as per references indicated in Hindu religious scriptures. In ancient times it was known by many names such as Saman tradition, or the religion of Nirgrantha or Jina.

Founder

About 2500 years ago Lord Mahävir (Vardhamän), the twenty fourth and the last Tirthankar of this era revived the same philosophy preached by his predecessor Lord Pärshva Näth in India. He expanded the code of conduct. The present Jain scriptures reflect only his preaching.

Major Scriptures

Lord Mahävir's preaching was orally compiled by his disciples in the Jain Ägam Sutras which consist of many texts.

The Ägam Sutras teach great reverence for all forms of life, strict codes of vegetarianism, asceticism, non-violence, and opposition to war. The existing Ägam Sutras were documented 1000 years after Lord Mahävir's Nirvana (1500 years ago). They are accepted as authentic preachings of Lord Mahävir by the Shvetämbar sect. The Digambar sect does not accept them as authentic.

The major Ägam Sutras are Ächäränga, Sutra_krutänga, Bhagavati, Dasvaikälik, Kalpa Sutra, and Uttarädhyayan Sutra. Digambars follow two main texts; Shatakhand Ägam and Kashäya Pähud, and four Anuyogas which consist of more than 20 texts. Digambar literature is written by great Ächäryas (scholars) from 100 to 1000 AD.

Sects

There are two major Sects:

- Digambar (sky clad) sect
- Shvetämbar (white cloth) sect

The Digambar monks wear no clothes, while Shvetämbar monks wear white clothes. Fundamentally the views of both sects on ethics and philosophy are identical.

The Shvetämbar sect is divided into three sub Sects:

- Shvetämbar Murtipujak sect (idol worship)
- Shvetämbar Sthänakaväsi sect (no idol worship)
- Shvetämbar Teräpanthi sect (no idol worship and a different interpretation of some principles)

Adherents

About six million, almost exclusively in India.

Goals

The primary goal of Jainism is to become a perfected soul, known as Siddha, Paramätmä, or God. The perfected soul is pure consciousness and possesses perfect knowledge, power, bliss, and omniscience.

This state is attained when all layers of Karma, which are viewed as substance, are removed causing the soul to rise to the ceiling of the universe, known as Moksha. The soul abides forever in solitary bliss in Moksha. In Jainism, Moksha is defined as liberation, self unity, solitaire, an endless calm, freedom from desire and ego, and freedom from birth, death, and rebirth. When it is reached, a human has fulfilled his destiny as a perfect being or God. Every living being has a potential to become God. For Jains, there is no creator God and therefore no communion with Him.

Path of Attainment

Right Perception (Samyak Darshan), Right Knowledge (Samyak Jnän), and Right Conduct (Samyak Chäritra) together leads to liberation. Right perception creates an awareness of reality or truth, right knowledge impels the person to proper action, and proper conduct leads him to the attainment of total freedom. They must coexist in a person if one is to make any progress on the path of liberation.

The soul passes through various stages of spiritual development, called Gunasthänas, which are progressive manifestations of the soul's innate faculties of perception, knowledge, and conduct. Jainism places great stress on non-violence (Ahimsä), multiplicity or pluralism of views (Anekäntaväda or Syädväda), non-possessions (Aparigraha) or limitation of possessions and non-possessiveness, asceticism, penance, yoga, and monasticism, as the means of attainment of liberation.

Synopsis

Jainism strives for the realization of the highest perfection of man, which in its original purity is free from all pain and the bondage of birth and death. The term Jain is derived from the Sanskrit word Jina, or conqueror and implies conquest over the self bondage of attachment and aversion.

Jains believe in God as pure soul characterized as all Knower and Observer but not Doer; therefore it is not accurate to state that they are atheists. Jains do not believe in a single supreme God who engages in providing and punishing to being and interfering in their matter. They believe that nature's law governs all affairs of an individual and all events of the universe.

Each living being (soul) is beginningless and endless, and eternally individual. It classifies souls into three broad categories: those that are not yet evolved, those in the process of evolution, and those that are liberated from birth and rebirth. The soul attains a better birth according to the amount of Karma it is able to eliminate during life. Between births, souls dwell in heaven, hell, humans, animals, birds, fish, vegetables etc. Its supreme ideal is non-violence (Ahimsä), equal kindness, and reverence for all forms of life in speech, thought, and action. Above all it is a religion of love and compassion to all living beings.

The vows taken by Jain monks and nuns are very severe. They involve the elements of asceticism which consist of various external and internal austerities. The external austerities acquire inner strength to stay unaffected by any kind of physical hardships or disease including staying on fast for any length of time until proper food is received, and non-possession of worldly items. The internal austerities constitute a Jain variety of Yoga, meditation, and non-attachment (or complete detachment) to worldly life.

Jainism is unique in allowing a very spiritually advanced person to move slowly towards his own death by certain practices (principally fasting) under specified circumstances. This is a voluntary act and is permitted only when a person is not capable of doing any austerities (removal of his own karma - Nirjarä) due to terminal illness / old age.

Beliefs

The spiritual lineage of the twenty-four Tirthankars (Jain Gods) of whom the ascetic sage Mahävir was the last. They should be revered and worshipped above all else.

God is not a Creator, a Destroyer, or a Savior. Such human conceptions are limited. All that may be said of Him is: He is. In other words He is pure consciousness, a perfected soul without any Karma attached to it. He is just a pure Knower and Observer.

The ultimate goal of every living being is eternal release from Samsär, the cycles of birth and death, which is known as liberation.

Each human soul is eternal and individual and each must conquer himself (his desires) by his own efforts in order to attain liberation (Moksha).

The path of liberation is to follow Right Perception, Right Knowledge, and Right Conduct. It can be achieved by following certain codes of conduct leading to proper ascetic discipline and strict religious observances. The Ägam Sutras are the sacred scriptures that guide moral and spiritual life to ultimately attain liberation.

The principle governing the successions of life is Karma. Our actions of body, mind, and speech bind us with Karma. One can get rid of

Karma by proper knowledge of the nine fundamental truths (nine Tattvas), self purification, penance, austerity, and meditation.

The sacredness of all life, that one must cease injuring sentient creatures, large and small, and that even unintentional killing bonds Karma. Non-violence is to be followed in action, thought, and speech and is the highest religion.

Symbols

Jainism uses many symbols to convey the message of its philosophy and practice. They consist of a digit of the Moon, three dots, the Swastika, OM, and the palm of a hand with the Chakra (wheel) inset. The symbol "Palm of a Hand" is most popular and widely known as the Jain religion symbol. The comprehensive Jain symbol was adopted in the year 1974, the year in which Jains celebrated the twenty fifth hundred years nirvana anniversary of Lord Mahävir. Each individual symbol is frequently used in Jainism.

- Palm:

    The Palm of the hand signifies this assurance, 'do not be afraid', indicating that human beings who are suffering due to karmic bondage do not need to be disheartened but have faith and change the course of their actions by treading the path of righteousness.

- Wheel:

    The Wheel of Dharma (Chakra) with 24 spokes represents the religion preached by the 24 Tirthankars consisting of non-violence (Ahimsä) in thought, words, and action. The word inside the wheel is Ahimsä. It is the distilled essence of the religion. The Sanskrit wording underneath translates as 'living beings render service to one another" or Compassionate Living - the very basis of our civilization.

- A digit of the Moon and Three Dots:

    The three Dots represent the Jain trinity: Right Perception (Samyak Darshan), Right Knowledge (Samyak Jnän), and Right Conduct (Samyak Chäritra), together they lead to liberation. The digit of the Moon represents the region wherein the liberated souls reside.

- Swastika (not shown):

  The Swastika signifies the cycles of births and deaths due to karma in any of the four regions of the non liberated soul. The non liberated soul takes birth in heaven, human, animal, and hell and suffers. It reminds one that he should follow the true religion and be liberated to get out of this suffering.

- OM (North American Jains have adopted OM instead of Swastika):

  Jain OM is made up of five letters a, a, aa, u, and m. The first letter "a" represents Arihanta (living God), the second "a" represents Ashariri (Siddha or perfected being), the letters "aa" represent Ächärya (head of congregation), the letter "u" represents Upädhyäy (monk teacher), and the letter "m" represents Muni (Sädhu or monks). Hence Jain OM represents the salutation to five revered personalities of Jain religion.

The overall symbol means that the living beings of the three worlds suffer from the miseries of transmigratory existence, can have recourse to the path of dharma shown by the Tirthankars, thereby bringing about auspiciousness for themselves, and after obtaining perfection, will live forever in the world of liberated souls.

Holidays

The dates of Jain holidays are determined by a lunar calendar adjusted to the solar seasons. Typically, the community gathers for worship - sometimes with drama, dance, and special sweets to mark events in the lives of the Tirthankars.

- Paryushan Parva - the holiest season - is an eight or ten-day period of fasting, complex rituals, review of Jain principles, and prayers for forgiveness from all living beings.

- Samvatsari Pratikraman - a detailed, three-hour ceremony of spiritual review and renewal of faith and forgiveness from other living beings. This ritual is performed on the last day of Paryushan Parva.

- Mahävir Jayanti - marks the birth of Lord Mahävir. Locally, this is an all day cultural event.

- Deepävali (Diwäli) – also known as Mahävir Nirvana day - marks the attainment of Liberation of Lord Mahävir.

- Akshaya Tritiya - marks the fast breaking day of a yearlong fast by the first Tirthankar Lord Rushabha. Jains who have been fasting on an alternate day for a year break their fast by drinking fresh sugar cane juice.

- Jnän Panchami – marks a Day of Knowledge – Jain scriptures are displayed in various religious places.

- Maun Ekädasi (Agiyäras) - This is the most pious day in a year. It marks many pious occasions such as Birth, Enlightenment, Nirvana of several Tirthankars.

The Guru's Cat

Each time the guru set for worship with his students the Äshram cat come in to distract them, so he ordered them to tie it when the Äshram was at prayer.

After guru died the cat continued to be tied at the worship time. And when the cat died, another cat was brought into the Äshram to make sure that guru's order was faithfully observed at worship time.

Centuries passed and learned treatises were written by the guru's scholarly disciples on the liturgical significance of tying up a cat while worship is performed.

Sikhism

Founded

About 500 years ago in Punjab, India.

Founder

Guru Nanak (1469 - 1539)

Major Scriptures

The main scripture "Ädi Granth" is revered as the living Guru of the faith.

Sects

The main sect is Khälsä. The other sects are the Ram Raiyäs, the Mandhäris, and Niränkäris. The Khälsä sect has no living Guru but the Mandhäris and Niränkäris sects have living Gurus.

Adherents

The population of the Sikh community is about 19 million and the majority live in India. Small communities of Sikhs also exist in the United Kingdom, Canada, the United States, Malaysia, and East Africa.

Goals

The goal of Sikhism lies in Moksha or salvation which is a union with God, and release into God's love, described as that of a lover with the beloved and resulting in self transcendence, egolessness, and enduring bliss. It is the fulfillment of individuality in which man, freed of all limitations, becomes coextensive and cooperant and copresent with God. In Sikhism, Moksha means release into God's love. Man is not God but fulfilled in unitary, mystical consciousness with Him. God is the personal Lord and Creator.

Path of Attainment

To lead humans to the goal of Moksha, Sikhism follows a path of Japa and hymns. Through the chanting of the holy names or Sat Näm, the soul is cleansed of its impurity, the ego is conquered, and the wandering mind is stilled. This leads to a super conscious stillness. From here the soul enters the divine light and thus attains a state of divine bliss.

Once this highest goal is attained, the devotee must devote his awareness to the good of others. The highest goal can be realized only by God's grace, and this is attained exclusively by following the true teacher (Sat Guru), and by repeating the holy names of the Lord guided by the Ädi Granth, the scripture and sole repository of spiritual authority. For Sikhs there is no deity worship and no symbol of divinity.

Synopsis

The word Sikhism is derived from Sikka meaning disciple. The movement was founded in the state of Punjab, India by Guru Nanak (1469 - 1539), who sought reconciliation of the Hindu and Muslim faiths in a middle path that embraced both. It united Hindu devotion (Bhakti) and Sufi (Islam) mysticism most successfully. He taught the unity of God, brotherhood of man, rejection of caste, and the futility of idol worship. He was followed by nine masters, the last of whom was Guru Gobind Singh (1666 - 1708; Guru 1675 - 1708).

The holiest place for Sikhs is the Golden Temple at Amritsar, Punjab, India. The fourth Guru, Rämdäs (Guru 1574 - 1581), founded it. The fifth guru Arjundev (Guru 1581 - 1606) gave Sikhism its holy book, the Granth Sahib or Ädi Granth, which contains hymns and writings of the first five Sikh gurus as well as those of Hindu and Muslim saints such as Kabir, Ravidäs, Surdäs, Farid, and Rämänand. Like Islam, Sikhs object to the worship of images. The sacred image is replaced by a large copy of the scripture – Guru Granth Sahib or Ädi Granth.

Sikhism began as a peaceful religion and patiently bore much persecution from the Muslims, but with Guru Gobind Singh, self-preservation forced a strong military aimed at protecting the faith and way of life against severe opposition.

Sikhism stresses the brotherhood of all men, rejection of caste differences, opposition to the worship of idols, the importance of devotion, intense faith in the Guru, and the repetition of God's Name (Näm) as a means of salvation.

There have been no Gurus in the Sikh tradition since Guru Gobind Singh, whose last instructions to his followers were to honor and cherish the teachings of the ten Gurus as embodied in the scripture, "Ädi Granth" also known as "Guru Granth Sahib". Since then Guru Granth has been the object of ultimate sanctity and the source of sacred inspiration; it is the highest authority for the Sikhs.

Sikhs are readily identifiable by their turbans. They take a vow not to cut their hair as well as not to smoke or drink alcoholic beverages. When Gobind Singh founded (1699) the martial fraternity Khälsä (pure), his followers vowed to keep the five K's (see Belief section). The ideal Sikh-man is a saint-warrior and avoids alcoholic drinks and tobacco. The noble mission of life is to serve one's family, to serve mankind, and finally to serve God.

Beliefs

God is the sovereign one, the omnipotent, immortal and personal creator. He is a being beyond time, who is called Sat Näm for His name is truth.

Man grows spiritually by living truthfully, serving selflessly, and by repetition of the holy name and Guru Nanak's prayer, Japaji.

Salvation lies in understanding the divine truth and that man's surest path to salvation lies in faith, love, purity, and devotion.

The scriptural and ethical authority of the Ädi Granth is God's revelation.

To know God, the Guru is essential as a guide, who is absorbed in love of the Real and is able to awaken the soul to its true and divine nature.

The world is Mäyä, a vain and transitory illusion. Only God is true as all else passes away.

The ten Sikh Gurus are all true teachers which are: Guru Nanak, Guru Angad, Guru Amardäs, Guru Rämdäs, Guru Arjundev, Guru Har Govind, Guru Har Räi, Guru Har Kishan, Guru Tegh Bahädur, and Guru Govind Singh.

Adopt the last name Singh, which means Lion, signifying courage.

Adopt the five symbols (five K's):

- Wear white soldier's short uniform (Kachha): signifies Purity
- Keep Sword (Kirpan): signifies Bravery
- Wear Iron Bracelet (Karä): signifies Morality
- Never cut hair and beard (Kesha): signifies Renunciation
- Keep Comb (Kangha) in hair: signifies Cleanliness

Symbols

The swords, shield, and dagger represent the martial spirit of the community. They signify that a Sikh must be prepared to fight and even sacrifice his life in defense of his faith.

Holidays

Sikhs follow a lunar calendar. All holidays follow a similar pattern of celebration such as worship and special food distribution.

- The dates for commemorating the birth day of each of the ten gurus are distributed throughout the year. Those of the founder (Guru Nanak) and of the tenth guru (Guru Gobind Singh) are especially important.
- Baisäki is a commemoration of the formation of the Khälsä sect in 1699.
- Guru Granth Sahib Day celebrates the proclamation that the Sikh scripture is the perpetual living Guru.

Mindfulness is waking up and living in harmony with oneself and with the world and appreciating the fullness of each moment of life.

Religions of the Far-East

SHINTOISM

CONFUCIANISM   TAOISM

Confucianism

Founded

Confucianism began 2,500 years ago in China.

Founder

Supreme Sage K'ung fu tsu (Confucius) and Second Sage Meng tzu (Mencius).

Major Scriptures

The Analects, Doctrine of the Mean, Great Learning, and writing of Mencius are the sacred books of Confucianism. The Analects contain the basic teachings and was compiled by the students of Confucius after his death. Because it was not written as a systematic philosophy, it contains frequent contradictions and many of the philosophical doctrines are ambiguous.

Sects

There are no formal sects within Confucianism. Followers are free to profess other religions yet still be Confucians.

Adherents

Estimated at 350 million, mostly in China, Japan, Burma and Thailand.

Goals

The primary goal of Confucianism is to create true nobility through proper education and the inculcation of all the virtues.

It is described as the return to the way of one's ancestors, and the classics are studied to discover the ancient way of virtue. Spiritual nobility is attainable by all men. It is perceived as a moral achievement.

Confucius accepted the Tao (see Taoism), but placed emphasis on the return to an idealized age and the cultivation of the superior man and on the pragmatic rather than the mystical. The superior man's greatest virtues are benevolent love, duty, wisdom, truth, and propriety. Salvation is seen as realizing and living one's natural goodness, which is endowed by heaven through education. The superior man always knows what is right and follows his knowledge.

Path of Attainment

Besides virtue, the five relationships offer the follower of Confucianism a means for progressing. These five relationships are ruler and ruled, father and child, husband and wife, older sibling and younger sibling, and friend and friend. Ancestors are revered in Confucianism, and it is assumed that their spirit survives death. With respect to a deity, Confucius himself was an agnostic, preferring to place emphasis on the ethical life here rather than to speak of a spiritual life beyond earthly existence; while guiding men's minds not to the future, but to the present and the past.

Synopsis

Confucianism, the philosophical system founded on the teaching of Confucius (551 - 479 BC), dominated Chinese socio-political life for most of Chinese history and largely influenced the cultures of Korea, Japan, and Indochina.

Confucianism is and has been for over 25 centuries, the dominant philosophical system in China and the guiding light in almost every aspect of Chinese life. Confucius and his followers traveled throughout many feudal states of the Chinese empire persuading rulers to adopt his social reforms. They did not offer a point by point program but stressed instead the way or "one thread" Jen, which is translated as humanity or love, that runs through all of Confucius' teachings. They urged individuals to strive for perfect virtue, righteousness (called i), and improvement of character.

Confucius was dedicated to the preservation of traditional ritual practices with an almost spiritual delight in its performance.

He taught the importance of harmony in the family, order in the state, and peace in the Empire. Teachings emphasize a code of conduct, self cultivation and propriety, and thus the attainment of social and national order. Stress is more on human duty and the ideal of the "superior man" than on a divine or supramundane reality. Still Confucius fasted, worshipped the ancestors, attended sacrifices, and sought to live in harmony with Heaven.

Beliefs

There is a presence of the Supreme Ruler in all things, and in Heaven as the ethical principle, whose law is order, impersonal and yet interested in mankind.

The purpose of life is to pursue an orderly and reverent existence in accord with "Li," propriety or virtue, so as to become the superior man.

The Golden Rule: Never do to others what you would not like them to do to you.

Confucius, China's first sage is the master of life whose teachings embody the most profound understanding of earth and Heaven, and that Mencius is China's second sage.

The writings of Confucius are a scriptural truth. The four sacred books are; The Analects, Doctrine of the Mean, Great Learning, and Writings of Mencius.

Each man has five relationships entailing five duties to his fellow man: to his ruler, to his parents and children, to his wife, to his brothers and sisters, and to his friend. The foremost is doing his familial duties.

Man is a master of his own life and fate, free to conduct himself as he wills, and that he should cultivate qualities of benevolence, righteousness, propriety, wisdom, and sincerity.

The family is the most essential institution among men, and religion should support the family and the state.

Symbols

This is the Chinese sign for Water. It symbolizes the life giving source.

Taoism

Founded

Taoism began about 2,500 years ago in China.

Founder

Sage Lao tzu is the founder to whom Confucius describes as a dragon riding the wind and clouds.

Major Scriptures

The Tao te Ching or Book of Reason and Virtue, is the shortest of all scriptures, containing only 5,000 words.

Sects

Taoism is a mystical tradition, so interpretations have been diverse and its sects are many.

Adherents

Estimated at 50 million, mostly in China and other parts of Asia.

Goals

The primary goal of Taoism may be described as the mystical intuition of the Tao, which is the way, the undivided unity, and the ultimate Reality. Both imminent and transcendent, the Tao is the natural way of all things, the nameless beginning of heaven and earth, and the Mother of all things.

All things depend upon the Tao, and all things return to it. Yet it lies hidden, transmitting its power and perfection to all things. He, who has realized the Tao, has arrived at pure consciousness and sees the inner truth of everything. Only one who is free of desire can apprehend the Tao, thereafter leading a life of "actionless activity."

There is no personal God in Taoism, and thus no union with Him. There are three worlds and all beings are within them. The worship is a part of the path.

Path of Attainment

One who follows the Tao follows the natural order of things, not seeking to improve upon nature or to manage virtue to others. The Taoist observes "wu wei" or non doing - like water seeks and finds its proper level without any effort. This path includes purifying oneself by stilling appetites and emotions. This is accomplished in part through meditation, breath control, and other forms of inner discipline, generally under a master. The foremost practice is goodness or naturalness, and detachment from worldly things.

Synopsis

The term Taoism refers both to the philosophy outlined in the Däode Jing (Tao Te Ching) (identified with Laozi or Lao tzu) and to China's ancient Taoist religion. Next to Confucianism, it ranks as the second major belief system in traditional Chinese thought.

Taoism is a Chinese philosophy and way of life dating back several millennia; codified around 500 B.C. Confucius told his students that in Lao Tzu he had met a dragon. Confucius favored a multiplicity of social roles and rules. By contrast, Taoism emphasizes intuition, spontaneity, and simplicity.

Three doctrines are particularly important to Taoist:

- Non being (wu):

    The creative force brings everything into being and the destructive force dissolves everything into non being.

- Return (fu):

    Everything, after completing its cycle, returns to non being.

- Non action (wu wei):

    Non action does not mean no action, but action in harmony

with nature, which is the best way to live life. If we keep still and listen to the inner prompting of the Tao, we shall act effortlessly and efficiently, hardly giving the matter a thought. We will be our true selves.

The prominent features of Taoist religion are belief in physical immortality, alchemy, breath control and hygiene (internal alchemy), a pantheon of deities, monasticism, and the ritual of community renewal, and revealed scriptures. Buddhism influenced the Taoist liturgy and theology.

The Tao, or the Way, has never been put down in words; rather it is left for the seeker to discover within himself. Lao tzu said, "The Tao that can be expressed or named is not the eternal Tao." Taoism is concerned with man's spiritual level of being. The awakened man is compared to bamboo; upright, simple, useful outside, and hollow inside. Radiant emptiness is the spirit of Tao, but no words will capture its spontaneity, or its eternal newness. The followers are taught to see the Tao everywhere, in all beings and in all things.

Taoist shrines are the homes of divine beings that guide the religion, bless and protect worshipers.

Zhuangzi taught that, from a purely objective viewpoint, all opposition are merely the creations of conceptual thought and imply no judgments of intrinsic value (one pole is no more preferable than its opposite). Hence, the wise person accepts life's inevitable changes.

Lie Xi said that the cultivation of Tao would enable a person to live for several hundred years. Taoism teaches the devotee to lead a long and tranquil life through the elimination of one's desires and aggressive impulses.

Beliefs

The Eternal may be understood as the Tao or the Way, which embraces the moral and physical order of the universe; the path of virtues; and the Absolute, understood as that "the Tao that can be described is not the eternal Tao".

The sage Lao Tsu is uniquely great as is his disciple Chuang Tsu.

The Tao te Ching and the writings of Chuang Tsu are important spiritual insights.

Man aligns himself with the Eternal when he observes humility, simplicity, gentle yielding, serenity, and effortless action.

The goal and the path of life are essentially the same, and that the Tao can be known only to exalted beings who realize it themselves -reflections of the beyond are of no avail.

The omniscient and impersonal Supreme is implacable beyond concern for human woe, but there exists lesser divinities, from the high gods who endure for eons the natural spirits and demons.

All actions create their opposing forces, and the wise will seek inaction in action.

Man is one of the Ten Thousand Things of manifestation; it is finite and will pass. Only Tao endures forever.

Tao believes in the oneness of all creation, in the spirituality of the material realms, and in the brotherhood of all men.

Symbols

The symbol of Taoism stands for what Taoist believe are the two basic forces Yang (male) and Yin (female) that mesh in a symbol of the Great Ultimate. The dark shape represents the Yin and the white shape represents the Yang. The Yin is the negative, passive, destructive principle, and the Yang is the positive, active, and constructive principle.

The dark area contains a white spot, the white area contains a dark spot, thereby indicating that no element is absolutely positive or negative, and each is within the other. The curving line between the *yin* and the *yang* signifies the golden mean or middle way, the life of harmony, ratio, and balance. The entire diagram is surrounded by a circle representing the Tao or the Absolute.

The Tao is the unchanging unity underlying changing plurality. It is the first all embracing principle from which all things are produced. It is indescribable and exists by itself.

Those who look outwards look in vain

Shintoism

Founded

Shinto is the indigenous religious tradition of Japan. Its roots lie deep in the prehistoric religious practices of the Japanese people. However, some believe that Shinto began around 2,500 - 3,000 years ago in Japan.

Founder

Shinto has no historical founder; however each of the 13 ancient sects believes it has its own founder.

Major Scriptures

Shinto does not have any canon of sacred scriptures, although important elements of its mythology and cosmology are found in Kojiki (Records of the Ancient) and Nilongi or Nikonshoki (ancient Japanese chronicles). The ritual hymns and prayers called Norito were compiled into written collections (Yengishki) at an early date.

Sects

There are two main divisions. One encompasses all thirteen ancient sects, which are very similar. The second is known as State Shinto. The State Shinto finds its highest expression in the worship of the Emperor and loyalty to the State and family.

Adherents

All Japanese participate in Shinto rites and many of them are also Buddhists. Hence, adherents are not a useful category for this religion. It is estimated that 30 million Japanese perform Shinto rites.

Goals

The primary goal of Shinto is to achieve a proper relationship (known as Kämi) with the ancestral beings. The Kämi is supernatural holy powers living in or connected to the world of the spirit. All living things can be Kämi. The human's nature is the highest for he possesses the most Kämi.

Path of Attainment

The proper relationship with ancestral beings is achieved in Shinto through observance of all taboos and the avoidance of such people and objects that might cause impurity or pollution. Prayers are made and offerings brought to the temples of the gods and goddesses, of which there are said to be a myriad of 800 in the universe. Man has no supreme God to obey, but only needs to know how to adjust to Kämi in its various manifestations. A person's Kämi (nature) survives death, and a man naturally desires to be worthy of being remembered with approbation by his descendants. Therefore, fulfillment of duties is a most important aspect of Shinto.

Synopsis

In the Chinese language, the word Shinto (Shin and Tao) signifies the way of the spirits or gods. It is called Kämi no michi in its native Japanese. The Kämi are innumerable Japanese deities that may be thought of as full fledged gods (such as the sun goddess Amaterasu, from whom the imperial family is said to descend); the divinized souls of great people (warriors, leaders, poets, scholars); the ancestral divinities of clans (Uji); the spirits of specific places, often of natural beauty (woods, trees, springs, rocks, mountains); or more abstractly, the forces of nature (fertility, growth, production).

Shinto shrines are over 100,000 in Japan. Kämi are generally worshiped at shrines (Jinjä) which are established in their honor. Worshipers will pass under a sacred arch (Torii) which helps demarcate the sacred area of the shrine. They will then purify themselves by washing their hands and rinsing their mouths, approach the shrine itself, make an offering, call on the deity, and utter a silent prayer. Fresh food, water, and incense are offered daily upon the altar. Special times for worship include important events like birth, youth, and marriage and festival dates (Matsuris) the New Year, the advent of spring, rice planting, midsummer, harvesting, and so on.

On any of these occasions the shrine will be crowded with worshipers, many of whom may wish to have their fortunes told or to receive special blessings or purifications from the Shinto priests. Certain shrines have also taken on national importance. The Grand Shrine of Ise, for example, is sacred to Amaterasu. Because, the sun goddess, is associated with the imperial family, her shrine is a national center of pilgrimage.

With the establishment of Buddhism in Japan during the Nara and Heian periods (AD 710 - 1185), Shinto quickly came under its influence as well as that of Confucianism and Chinese culture as a whole. On the one hand, it became more highly structured, following the Buddhist lead. On the other hand, certain Kämi came to be thought of as manifestations of particular Buddhas or Bodhisattvas. For example, Amaterasu was identified with the cosmic Buddha Vairocana. Thus the two religions both mixed and coexisted at the same time.

There is an inward belief in the sacredness of the whole universe, and that man can be in tune with this sacredness. Stress is placed on truthfulness and purification through which man may remove the "dust" which conceals his inherently divine nature and thus receive the guidance and blessings of Kämi. The Shintoist's ardent love of the motherland has found unique expression in the loyalty and devotion of the Japanese people to their state.

Beliefs

The Way of the Gods (Kämi no Michi) asserts nature's sacredness and uniquely reveals the supernatural.

There is no single supreme being but a myriad of gods which are superior beings. They are among all the wonders of the universe which is not inanimate but filled everywhere with sentient life.

Believe in Scriptural authority of the great books known as the Records of Ancient Matters (Kojiki), Chronicles of Japan (Nikonshoki), and Collection of 10,000 Leaves containing ritual hymns and prayers (Yengi Shiki).

The State is a divine institution whose laws should not be disobeyed and to which individuals must sacrifice their own needs.

The sanctity of cleanliness and purity of body and spirit, and that impurity is a religious transgression.

Shintoists believe in moral and spiritual uprightness as the cornerstone of religious ethics and in the supreme value of loyalty to all your acts.

The supernatural reveals itself through all that is natural and beautiful, and these are more valuable than philosophical or theological doctrines.

Everything is a divine Spirit, that the world is one brotherhood, that all men are capable of deep affinity with the Divine, and that there exists no evil in the world.

Shintoist believe in the practical use of ceremony and ritual, and in the worship of the deities that animate nature, including the Sun Goddess, the Star God, and the Storm God.

Symbols

A wooden gate called Torii is the symbol of Shintoism. The word Shinto is derived from "Shen Tao" which means the "Way of the gods." A Torii stands at the entrance of a Shinto temple. It consists of two posts connected by crossbars. The posts represent pillars that support the sky, and the crossbar symbolizes the earth.

Why Good People Die

The village preacher at the home of an elderly parishioner was busy answering grandma's questions over a cup of coffee.

"Why does the Lord send us epidemics every so often?" asked the grandma.

"Well," said the preacher, "sometimes people become so wicked they have to be removed and so the good Lord allows the coming of epidemics."

"But then," objected grandma, "why do so many good people get removed with the bad?"

"The good ones are summoned for witness," explained the preacher. "The Lord wants to give every soul a fair trial."

There is nothing that the Rigid Believer cannot find an explanation for.

Religions of the West

CHRISTIANITY   JUDAISM

BAHÄ'I

ISLAM   ZOROASTRIANISM

Judaism

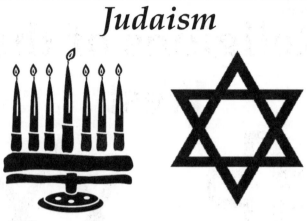

Founded

Judaism began about 3,700 years ago in Canaan which now contains the State of Israel, Palestine and Jordan.

Founder

Abraham is the father of the Hebrew people (Jews). God established His covenant with Moses who emancipated the enslaved Jewish tribes from Egypt.

Sects

Jews are divided into Orthodox, Conservative and Reform groups with other regional and ethnic divisions.

Major Scriptures

The basic source of Jewish belief is the Hebrew Bible (called the "Old Testament" by Christians). Its first five books are called the Torah or the Pentateuch of Moses. Torah means 'law and teaching'. The five books are Genesis, Exodus, Levicus, Numbers, and Deuteronomy. The Torah was traditionally regarded as the primary revelation of God and his law to humanity to his spokesman Moses on Mount Sinai. It is considered eternal truth. Its laws were clarified and elaborated in the oral Torah, or the tradition of the elders, and were eventually written down in the Mishnah and Talmud. Jewish literature on legal, ethical, philosophic, mystical, and devotional is virtually endless.

Adherents

There are about 14 million Jews worldwide; over half in the U.S.

Goals

The goal of Judaism lies in the strict obedience to God which can alleviate the plight of the individual and of society, bringing rewards in the future life when the Messiah will come to overthrow evil and reward the righteous in God's kingdom on earth, the Day of the Lord. The soul thereafter will enjoy God's presence and love forever.

Path of Attainment

Man has two impulses; good and evil. He can either follow God's law or rebel and be influenced by Satan, who caused God's creation to go astray. To follow God's law is the highest morality, possible through obedience to the Torah, which pleases God. One must follow justice, charity, ethics and honesty, being true to the one true God, Yahweh. Judaism teaches that all people are created in God's image and deserve to be treated with dignity and respect.

Synopsis

The religion of the Jews is inseparable from their history as a people. By far the most profound characteristic of Judaism is its strict monotheism. The Jews hold an unshakable belief in one God and one God only, called Yahweh, from whom all creation flows. Jews typically do not refer to God as Yahweh.

Much of the Torah traces the ancestry of Abraham through Isaac, Jacob, Joseph, and finally to Moses, the foremost of God's prophets in Hebrew history. Moses gave Judaism the Ten Commandments and established the religious laws and traditions. Jews must also observe over 400 laws in addition to the Ten Commandments.

The Ten Commandments for Worship and Conduct taken from Exodus 20:3:14:

- You shall have no other gods besides Me.
- You shall not make for yourself a sculptured image, or any likeness of what is in the heavens above, or on earth below, or in the waters under the earth. You shall not bow down to them or serve them.

- You shall not swear falsely by the name of the Lord, your God.

- Remember the Sabbath day and keep it holy. The Lord blessed the Sabbath day and hallowed it.

- Honor your father and your mother.

- You shall not murder.

- You shall not commit adultery.

- You shall not steal.

- You shall not bear false witness against your neighbor.

- You shall not covet your neighbor's house, wife, male or female slave, ox or his ass, or anything that is your neighbor's.

The first four commandments are on religious belief and worship; the other commandments are on proper conduct and relationships with others.

The Jewish people consider themselves a chosen people apart from all the other people of the earth by virtue of their covenant with Yahweh (God). They do not believe that they were chosen for any special privileges but rather have the responsibility to bring God's message to humanity by living a good moral life and obeying the laws of the Torah.

Much stress is placed on the hallowing of daily existence, worship in the synagogue, prayer and reading of the scriptures. Few religions can boast of such a close knit family tradition as Judaism, making the home a great strength to the religion and a constant refuge to the faithful. Each day, morning and evening, every devout Jew affirms his faith by repeating Moses' prayer, "Hear O Israel the Lord our God, the Lord is One".

Judaism has a system of law, known as Halachah, regulating civil and criminal justice, family relationships, personal ethics and manners, social responsibilities such as help to the needy, education, and community institutions as well as worship and other religious observances.

Individual practices still widely observed include the dietary laws (Kosher); rules concerning marital relationship, daily prayer and study; and the recital of many blessings, especially before and after meals. The Sabbath and festivals are observed both in the home and in the

Synagogue, a unique institution for prayer and instruction that became the model for the church in Christianity and for the mosque in Islam.

The Sabbath, from sunset Friday to sunset Saturday, is the day of rest which is a unique gift of God. It is observed by refraining from work, by attending a synagogue service, and by special food. Friday evening is marked in the home by the lighting of a lamp or candles by the woman of the household, the recital of the Kiddish (a ceremonial blessing affirming the sanctity of the day) over a cup of wine, and the blessing of children by parents. The end of the Sabbath is marked by parallel ceremonies called Havdalah. Similar home ceremonies occur on the other festivals.

The holidays prescribed in the Torah are the two "days of awe," Rosh Hashanah (New Year) and Yom Kippur (Day of Atonement), and three joyous festivals; Passover, Shavuoth (Feast of Weeks), and the Feast of Tabernacles. Later additions are the festive occasions of Chanukah and Purim, and the fast of the Ninth of Av (Tishah be Av), commemorating the destruction of the Temple.

Later on according to many biblical scholars, some elements of the Persian religion were incorporated into Judaism: a more elaborate doctrine of Angels; the figure of Satan; and a system of beliefs concerning the end of time, including a predetermined scheme of world history, a final judgment, and the Resurrection of the dead. These ideas were expounded in many visionary documents called Apocalypses; none of them were included in the Hebrew Bible except in the Book of Daniel.

Beliefs

In the One God and Creator who is incorporeal and transcendent, beyond the limitation of form yet who cares for the world and its creatures, rewarding the good and punishing the evil. One God is referred to as the God of Abraham, Isaac, and Jacob.

In the Prophets of which Moses was God's foremost, and the Ten Commandments revealed to him by God on Mount Sinai as man's highest law.

No priest should intervene in the relationship of man and God, nor should God be represented in any form, nor should any being be worshipped other than the One God, Yahweh.

That upon death the soul goes to Heaven (or to Hell first if it has been sinful), that one day the Messiah will appear on earth and there will be a Day of Judgment, and the dead shall physically arise to Life Everlasting.

The universe is not eternal. It was created by God and will be destroyed by Him.

In man's spiritualization through adherence to the law, justice, charity, and honesty.

In the Torah as God's word and scripture, composed of the five Old Testament books. They are God's only immutable law.

That God has established a unique spiritual covenant with the Hebrew people to uphold for mankind the highest standards of monotheism and piety.

In the duty of the family to make the home a House of God through devotion and rituals, prayers, sacred festivals, and observation of the Holy Days.

Symbols

The seven branched Menorah is a familiar sign for Judaism. The Menorah is a representation of the creation of the world by God. According to Genesis of the Old Testament, God created the world in six days and rested on the seventh day. The middle light indicates the Sabbath (last day of the week), a holy day, and a day of rest.

The light of the candles symbolizes the presence of God or Shekinah within the temple. The Menorah with its golden branches and flaming candles signifies the undying and inexhaustible spirit of Judaism.

The Star of David is the symbol of Judaism and of Israel. It consists of two triangles that interlace and form a six pointed star. It represents the six tribes of Israel. In Hebrew, the symbol is called the Magen David, which means the Shield of David.

Holidays

The Jewish religious calendar, of Babylonian origin, consists of 12 lunar months, amounting to about 354 days. Six times in a 19 year cycle a 13th month is added to adjust the calendar to the solar year (similar to the Hindu and Jain calendar).

Hence holiday dates vary every year but their solar seasons do not. A day is reckoned from sunset to sunset.

Some Jewish holidays are mandated by Torah; others mark major historical events.

- Rosh Hashanah (New Year) - early autumn - commemoration of the creation of the world, marked by abstaining from work.
- Hanukkah (Feast of Dedication) - an eight-day festival in December celebrates the rededication of the Temple after its rescue from desecration by Judas Maccabeus during the rule of Antiochus.
- Pesach (Passover) - a week-long spring remembrance of the Exodus from slavery in Egypt. Most Jews abstain from eating yeast-breads and enjoy Seders - ritual meals with a menu laden with symbolism.

Humanity

Much advance publicity was made for the address the Master would deliver on "The Destruction of the World" and a large crowd gathered at the monastery grounds to hear him. The address was over in less than a minute. All he said was:

These things will destroy the human race:

Politics without Principle

Progress without Compassion

Wealth without Work

Learning without Silence

Religion without Fearlessness

Worship without Awareness

Act of Sinning

The Arab mystic, Abu Hassan Bushanja, says, "The act of sinning is not so harmful as the desire and the thought of it. It is one thing for the body to indulge in pleasure for a moment, and quite another for the mind and heart to chew on it endlessly.

Each time I chew on the sins of others, I suspect the chewing gives me greater pleasure than the sinning gives the sinner.

Zoroastrianism

Founded

Zoroastrianism began 2,600 years ago in Persia.

Founder

Spenta Zarathushthra (628 - 551 BC) known as Prophet Zoroaster.

Major Scriptures

The sacred literature of Zoroastrianism is the Zend Avesta (Persian), which was compiled about 800 years later during the Sassanian period (AD 224 640) from much earlier materials. Only a portion of the Zend Avesta remains, but the language of its earliest sections is extremely ancient, closely related to the Hindu Vedäs.

Sects

There are two main sects. They have split over a question of the religious calendar.

Adherents

About 125,000 living mostly near Bombay, India where they are called Pärsis.

Goals

The goal of Zoroastrianism is to be rewarded with a place in heaven where the soul will be with God (known as Ähurä Mäzdä), while sharing His blessed existence forever.

Path of Attainment

Man's life is a moral struggle, not a search for knowledge or enlightenment. He is put on the earth to affirm and approve the world, not to deny it, and not to escape from it. Salvation is found in obedience to the will of Ähurä Mäzdä as revealed and taught by His prophet Zoroaster. Man has only one life. He also has the freedom to choose between good and evil. Evil is embodied in Angra Mainyä who rebelled against God. At death, each is judged and consigned to his deserved abode.

Zoroastrians hold truth as the greatest virtue, followed by good thoughts, words, and deeds. They place high value on an ethical life. Though there is a resurrection of the dead, a judgment day, and a kingdom of heaven on earth, followed by punishment of the wicked, all sins are eventually burned away and all of humankind exists forever with God - Ähurä Mäzdä. Hell is not eternal.

Synopsis

The religion of ancient Iran was derived from that of the ancient Indo Europeans, or Aryans. The language of the earliest Zoroastrian writings is close to that of the Indian Vedäs, and much of the mythology is recognizably the same.

Linguistic evidence suggests that Prophet Zoroaster was born in northeastern Iran. Zoroastrianism became the official religion of the Achaemenid Empire. Its theology and cosmology may have influenced the development of Greek, later Jewish, Christian, and Muslim thought. The Muslim conquest of Iran during the 7th century AD marked the beginning of a steady decline of Zoroastrianism. Persecution resulted in the migration (about the 10th century AD) of the majority of Zoroastrians to India, where the Pärsis of Bombay are their modern descendants.

The rituals of Zoroastrianism revolve around devotion to good and battle against the forces of evil. The powers of good are led by Ähurä Mäzdä (the Wise Lord) and the forces of evil by Angra Mainyä or Ahriman (the Evil Spirit). In order to combat evil one must oppose the forces of evil at all times and the people who side with them. Good will eventually triumph on Judgment Day, when a Messiah and Savior named Sayoshant will appear to punish the wicked and establish the righteous in a paradise on Earth.

The maintenance of life is the most important principle which forms the basis of Zoroastrian ethics. In order to maintain life one must till the soil, raise cattle, marry, and have children. Asceticism and celibacy are condemned. Purity and avoidance of defilement (from death, demons and the like) are valued.

A central feature of the faith is the sacred fire that is constantly kept burning in every home which is fueled by fragrant sandalwood. Fire is considered the only worshipful symbol. It is seen as the manifestation of the truth of Ähurä Mäzdä, as preached by Prophet Zoroaster. It is the great purifier and sustainer, and is of the nature of the Sun itself. Also important is the ritual drink, Haoma, which is related to the Vedic Soma.

Beliefs

There are two great beings in the universe, Ähurä Mäzdä, who created man and all that is good, beautiful, and true; and Angra Mainyä, who vivifies all that is evil, ugly, and destructive.

Man has a free will to align himself with good or evil, and when all mankind is in harmony with the God Ähurä Mäzdä, Angra Mainyä will be conquered.

Zoroaster is the foremost Prophet of God and the Zend Avesta has the scriptural authority.

God may best be worshipped through the representation of fire. He has Seven Personalities:

- Eternal Light
- Right and Justice
- Goodness and Love
- Strength of Spirit
- Piety and Faith
- Health and Perfection
- Immortality

The soul is immortal and upon death crosses over Hell by a narrow bridge. The good cross safely to Heaven and the evil fall into Hell.

Sayoshant, a savior who was born of a virgin, will appear at the end of time reviving the dead, rewarding the good, and punishing the evil. Thereafter Ähurä Mäzdä will reign.

Purity is the first virtue, truth the second, and charity the third. Man must discipline himself by good thoughts, words, and deeds.

Marriage excels chastity (continence), action excels contemplation, and forgiveness excels revenge.

Symbols

The Caldron of Fire is the symbol of Zoroastrianism. Fire burns away all evil and it can never be impure. Fire represents God and typifies the divine spark within.

The maintenance of a sacred fire in fire temples called Atar Beheram without allowing it to be extinguished, is an important feature of Zoroastrianism. It is treated like a king with a crown hung over it. The Priests feed it five times a day at prescribed hours. Offering of sandalwood is considered meritorious for donors.

Holidays

Zoroastrians worship the one transcendent and immanent Deity Ähurä Mäzdä, who is symbolized by a sacred fire and make offerings to the sacred fire.

Celebrates various Stages of Divine creation:

- Divine Spirit Khshathra Vairya [Power], creator and protector of the Sky (April)
- Divine Spirit Haurvatat [Wholeness], creator and protector of Water (June-July)
- Divine Spirit Spenta Armaiti [Devotion], creator and protector of Earth (September)
- Divine Spirit Ameretat [Immortality], creator and protector of Vegetation (October)
- Divine Spirit Asha Vahishta [Righteousness], creator and protector of fire (March) Also Zoroastrian New Year (Naw Ruz)
- Divine Spirit Vohu Manah [Good Intent], creator and protector of Animals (Vohu Manah is one of seven male and female divine emanations of Deity Ähurä Mäzdä) (December – January)
- Divine Spirit Spenta Mainyu [Holy Spirit], creator and protector of humans (March)

Day commemorating the death of Zoroastrian Prophet Zarathushthra

Christianity

Founded

Christianity began about 2,000 years ago in Canaan.

Founder

Christianity is based on the teachings of Jesus of Nazareth (Jesus Christ), believed to be the Son of God. He died in Jerusalem in 33 AD.

Major Scriptures

The Christian Bible consists of the

- Old Testament (39 Books of Hebrew Bible) which records God's covenant with the Jewish people. It is written in Hebrew.

- New Testament (27 Books) which records Christ's life and teachings. It is written in Greek and dates from 50 AD. Jesus himself left no writings. He chose 12 apostles to preach His doctrine.

Some sects (Catholic and some Protestants) also recognize additional 7 Books of the Apocrypha. It also contains a collection of the early Christian writings proclaiming Jesus as the Lord and Savior.

Sects

Christianity is divided into three main sects; Roman Catholic, Eastern Orthodox, and Protestant. Among Protestants there are over 2,000 smaller sects, including Lutherans, Presbyterians, Baptists, Methodists, Congregationalists, and Unitarians.

Adherents

Over 1 billion, the largest of world religions, is represented in most areas of the world.

Goals

The goal of Christianity is eternal life with God in heaven, a perfect existence in which God's glory and bliss are shared. It is also a personal life, enjoyed differently by individuals according to the amount of grace received and accepted in life.

Path of Attainment

Man's plight is caused by disobedience to God's will as revealed in the law of God found in the Bible. God's justice demands that penalty must be paid for that disobedience. That penalty was paid by God himself taking on the human flesh in the person of Jesus and dying the ignominious and completely undeserved death of a criminal on a cross. By this sacrificial act, God, out of sheer grace and love made it possible for all those who believe in the saving power of this act to have credit to their account the complete and perfect obedience of Jesus so that God regards them the same as if they had never sinned.

Jesus' resurrection from the dead is proof of God's power over sin, death, and proof that he can save in this way. Those who accept God's gift of salvation are empowered by the Holy Spirit to begin to live a life of increasing virtue and obedience to God and in this way show their gratitude to God for freeing them from the guilt of their sins.

The good Christian lives a life of virtue and obedience to God out of gratitude to God for sacrificing Jesus for the sins of all who come to accept Jesus Christ as their personal Savior and Lord. Jesus is to return again to judge the world and bring God's rule to earth. Through following the law of God as found in the Holy Bible and through God's grace, man attains salvation.

Synopsis

Christianity is the religion of about a billion people whose belief system centers on the teachings of Jesus Christ. Christians believe that the original human beings rebelled against God and from that time until the coming of Christ the world was ruled by Sin. Jesus of Nazareth was and is the Messiah or Christ promised by God in the prophecies of the Old Testament (the Hebrew Bible). By his life, death, and Resurrection Jesus freed those who believe in him from their sinful state and made them recipients of God's saving Grace. Many also await the Second Coming of Christ, which they believe will complete God's plan of salvation.

The majority of Christians adhere to the Apostles' Creed:

- I believe in God, the Father Almighty, Maker of Heaven and Earth.

- I believe in Jesus Christ, His only Son, our Lord. Who was born of the Virgin Mary by the power of the Holy Spirit, suffered under Pontius Pilate, was crucified, dead and buried. He descended into hell. The third day He rose again from the dead. He appeared to his disciples, commanding them to spread the good news of salvation from sin and death to all people. He ascended unto Heaven and Sitteth on the right hand of God, the Father Almighty. From thence, He shall come to judge the living and the dead.

- I believe in the Holy Spirit (Ghost), the communion of saints, the forgiveness of sins, the resurrection of the body, and the life everlasting.

Christians are monotheists (believers in one God). The early church, however, developed the characteristic Christian doctrine of the Trinity, in which God is thought of as a Creator (Father), a Redeemer (Son), and a Sustainer (Holy Spirit), but one God in essence.

Christians worship in congregations, celebrate baptism (an individual's entrance into Christianity) and the Eucharist (Holy Communion), which represents Jesus' Last Supper with his disciples. Christianity has an unswerving belief that it is the only true religion, the only path to salvation. This engenders a missionary zeal, an urgency to evangelize around the world. Stress is placed on acceptance of Jesus as God and Savior, on good conduct, compassion, and service to humanity, faith, and preparation for the Final Judgment. Only good Christians will be saved.

Substantial differences in faith exist among the various churches. Those in the Protestant tradition insist on Scriptures as the sole source of God's Revelation. The Roman Catholics give greater importance to the tradition of the church in defining the content of faith, believing it to be divinely guided in its understanding of scriptural revelation. They stress the role of ecumenical councils in the formulation of the doctrine. In Roman Catholicism, the Pope is regarded as the final authority in matters of belief. A prominent feature of the Roman Catholic and Orthodox churches is Monasticism.

The Roman Catholic and Orthodox churches have an all-male threefold ministry of bishops, priests, deacons, and several minor orders. The Roman Catholic Church is headed by the Pope. In the Orthodox churches and those of the Anglican Communion (which retain the threefold ministry) major decisions are made by the bishops acting as a group with lay consultation, sometimes with votes. Church government among Lutherans, Reformed, and other Protestants generally involves the laity even more fully, with the policy being determined either by local congregations or by regional assemblies composed of both clergy and lay people. Most Protestant churches, including some provinces of the Anglican Communion, now permit the ordination of women.

Ten Commandments from the King James Version of the Bible:

- I am the Lord thy God
- Thou shalt have no other gods before me
- Thou shalt not make unto the any graven images
- Thou shalt not take the name of the Lord thy God in vain
- Remember to keep the Sabbath day holy
- Honor thy father and thy mother
- Thou shalt not kill
- Thou shalt not commit adultery
- Thou shalt not steal
- Thou shalt not bear false witness against thy neighbor. Thou shalt not covet thy neighbor's house, covet thy neighbor's wife, covet thy neighbor's manservant, and covet thy neighbor's maidservant, ox, or ass

Beliefs

In God, the Creator of the universe, reigning forever distinct over man, his beloved creation.

God exists as three persons; Father, Son, and Holy Spirit or Ghost and these three are one infinite, eternal, holy God, the same in substance, equal in power and glory (Holy Trinity).

In the Messiah: that God sent his Son Jesus Christ to show people the way God wants them to live.

That Jesus Christ was born of Mary, a virgin. He was crucified on the cross then resurrected from the dead and now sits at the right hand of the Father as the final judge of the dead and that He will return again as prophesied.

That Salvation can be achieved through Jesus Christ, who died and rose to reveal God's love and plan for humanity.

In the historical truth of the Holy Bible, that it is a sacred scripture of the highest authority and the only word of God.

Satan exists and is the chief agent of evil, deception and darkness in this world.

Man is born a sinner, and that he may know salvation only through the savior, Jesus Christ, God's only begotten son.

That the soul is embodied for a single lifetime, but is immortal and accountable to God for all thoughts and actions.

That upon death the soul enters Heaven, Purgatory (Roman Catholics belief) or Hell according to its earthly deeds and its acceptance of the Christian faith. There awaiting the Last Judgment when the dead shall rise again, the redeemed to enjoy life everlasting and the unsaved to suffer eternally.

In the intrinsic goodness of humanity and the affirmative nature of life and in the priceless value of love, charity and faith.

Thou shalt love thy neighbor as thyself.

Golden Rule: Do unto others as you would have others do unto you.

Symbols

The cross is the symbol of Christianity. Jesus Christ, the founder of the Christian faith died on a cross in ancient Palestine. Jesus died to save humankind. It represents the self sacrifice and love of Christ for humanity.

Holidays

The holidays celebrate the events in the life of Jesus Christ.

- Christmas - The birth of Jesus Christ is commemorated on Christmas and is almost universally celebrated.

- Easter - The resurrection of Christ is commemorated at Easter (early spring) on Saturday night and a festival service on Easter Sunday morning. Hence Sunday, the day of Christ's resurrection, is observed as a time of rest and worship.

- All Saints Day is important for many Christians. Some give special reverence to Mary (Jesus' Mother) and other saints on particular days. Some observe Reformation Day, or events related to their branch.

An Ancient Christian Legend

When the Son of God was nailed to the cross and died, he went straight down to hell and set free all the sinners there in torment.

And the Devil wept and wailed for he thought he would get no more sinners for hell.

The God said to him, "Do not weep, for I shall send you all those who are self-righteous in their condemnation of sinners. And hell will fill up again till I return."

Islam

Founded

About 1,400 years ago in Arabia.

Founder

Prophet Mohammed (early 7th century)

Many Muslims believe that Prophet Mohammed is not the "founder" of Islam but he received the divine revelations recorded in the Qur'an during his life (570 - 632 AD). They regard that their religion is the restoration of the original religion of Abraham (Judaism) through the Prophet Mohammed in the 7th century. They would also stress that Islam is a timeless religion, not just because of the eternal truth that it proclaims but also because it is every person's religion, the natural religion in which every person is born.

Major Scriptures

The Qur'an is God's Speech written in Arabic. It is the sacred book of Islam explained as the religion of Abraham. In the Qur'an, Abraham is the patriarch who turned away from idolatry, who came to his Lord with an undivided heart, who responded to God in total obedience when challenged to sacrifice his son, and who served God uncompromisingly.

Sects

There are two main divisions within Islam. The Sunnis are followers of the political successors of Mohammed. The Shiites are followers of Mohammed's family successors all martyred at an early age.

Adherents

About 950 million mostly in the Middle East, Pakistan, Bangladesh, Africa, China, Indonesia, Central Asia, and India. Today Islam is the world's fastest growing religion.

Goals

The primary goal of Islam is to enjoy eternal life, both physical and spiritual in heaven with Allah (means God in Arabic). Heaven is a paradise in which all joys and pleasures abound and in which one lives amid beautiful gardens enjoying all comforts. Man is the noblest creation of God, ranking above the angels.

Path of Attainment

Total submission to Allah is the single path to salvation, and even that is no guarantee, for Allah may desire even a faithful soul to experience misery. The good Muslim surrenders all pride, sins, and follows explicitly the will of Allah as revealed in the Qur'an by His last and greatest prophet, Mohammed. This and this alone brings a full and meaningful life and avoids the terrors of hell, which befalls sinners and infidels.

Muslims believe in the five doctrines and observe the five pillars. The virtues of truthfulness, temperance and humility before God are foremost for Islam, and the practices of fasting, pilgrimage, prayer and charity are most necessary to please Allah.

Synopsis

Islam means submission, surrender to the Will of Allah. Islam also means peace. Those who submit are called Muslims.

The Qur'an records that Mohammed was the Seal of the Prophets, the last of a line of God's messengers that began with Adam (first man created by God) and included Abraham, Noah, Moses, and Jesus. Mohammed left the Word of God for the future guidance of the community revealed to him and recorded in the Qur'an, and the Sunnä, the collective name for his life and teachings as recorded in the traditional literature (Hädith).

Islam recognizes God's sending of messengers to all people and his granting of "Scripture and Prophethood" to Abraham and his descendants which results in the awareness of a very special link between Muslims, Jews, and Christians as all Abraham's children.

The Qur'an mentions, among others, Abraham and his sons, Solomon and the queen of Sheba, and the disciples of Jesus. The Muslims also recognize earlier Scriptures, namely, the Taurat (Torah) given to Moses, the Zabur (Psalms) of David, and the Injil (Gospel) of Jesus.

Islamic doctrines are commonly discussed and taught widely under six headings:

- God: the sole creator, the One and Only
- Angels: servants of God, play an important role in the daily life of Muslims
- Scriptures: God's speech
- Messengers: God's message revealed through His Messengers
- The Last Day: every soul will stand-alone and will have to account for its deeds
- Predestination: the divine initiative is all decisive in bringing humans to faith ("had God not guided us, we had surely never been guided," 7:43)

When applied to Islam, the word religion has a far more comprehensive meaning than it commonly has in the West. Islam encompasses personal faith and piety, the creed and worship of the community of believers, a way of life, a code of ethics, a culture, a system of laws, an understanding of the function of the state, in short, guidelines and rules for life in all its aspects and dimensions.

Islam teaches absolute monotheism and Mohammed's primacy as the last Prophet. Stress is on the brotherhood of believers, non difference of religious and secular life, obedience to God's Law, abstinence from alcohol, good conduct, and the limitation of all except Allah. Islam is based upon five pillars or principle acts of faith to which every Muslim in the world adheres.

- Faith in Allah (Shahada): there is no God but God (Allah) and Mohammed is God's Prophet or Messenger (in Arabic – la – illalah il-lalah ud Muhammedun rdsulon).
- Ritual Prayer (Salat): perform five times a day facing Mecca the
- Alms Giving (Zakät): support the mosque and the poor

- Fasting (Säwm): throughout Ramadän, the ninth month of the Muslim calendar, the faithful fast (abstaining from food and drink) from sunrise to sunset.

- Pilgrimage (Hajj): At least once in a lifetime every believer must go to Mecca, the holy city. They go dressed in simple, seamless white garments. This is the binding force of the people who have embraced Islam.

According to Muslims, the Sharia (the way, denoting the sacred law governing the life of individuals as well as the structures of society) is derived from four sources

- The Qur'an, the holy scripture

- The Sunnä (customs) of the Prophet, which are embodied in the Hädith (tradition)

- Qiyas (analogy) the application of a decision of the past, or the principles on which it was based, to new questions

- Jma (consensus) the consensus of the community of believers, who, according to a saying of the Prophet, would not agree on any error

After the death of the Prophet Mohammed, a series of successors (Khalifä, or Caliphä, or IMAM) were chosen to rule in his place.

The interpretations of Jihäd (striving in the way of God), sometimes added as an additional duty, vary from sacred war to striving to fulfill the ethical norms and principles expounded in the Qur'an.

Beliefs

Allah is the Supreme Creator and Sustainer, all knowing and transcendent and yet the arbiter of good and evil, the final judge of humans.

The five Pillars of Faith:

- Faith in the only God Allah and His Prophet Mohammed
- Praying five times daily
- Charity through alms giving
- Fasting during Ramadän, the ninth month of the Islam calendar
- Pilgrimage to the Holy city Mecca

The Qur'an is the Word of God and the sacred scripture mediated through the Angel Gabriel to the Prophet Mohammed.

The direct communion of each man with God, all are equal in the eyes of God and therefore priests or other mediators are not needed.

The pure transcendence of God, great beyond imagination, no form or idol can be worshipped in His Name.

The soul of a man is immortal, embodied once on earth then entering Heaven or Hell upon death according to his conduct and faith on earth.

In the Last Judgment and that man should stand in humble awe and fear of God's wrathful and vengeful power.

That truthfulness should be observed in all circumstances, although it may bring injury or pain.

That salvation is only obtained through God's Grace and not through man's efforts yet he should do all good and avoid all sins, especially drunkenness, usury, and gambling.

Symbols

The moon gives cool and soothing light to a weary traveler on the hot sands of Arabia and the stars guide him towards his destination. The religion of Islam also gives cool light and solace to the weary traveler on the scorched paths of worldly life and guides him towards Allah, the Supreme God.

Holidays

Islam uses a non-adjusting lunar calendar which numbers the years from the migration to Medina. Holidays shift through the solar seasons. The two major holidays are:

- Id-ul-Fitr marks the breaking of the fast of Ramadän by giving charity to the needy, additional mid-morning prayer, visits with friends and family, and exchanging gifts.
- Id-ul-Adha is the festival of sacrifice at the conclusion of the Hajj. It commemorates the willingness of the prophet Abraham to sacrifice his son Ishmael in obedience to God's command. Animals are sacrificed, and part of the meat is offered to the needy. The day includes special prayer, family gatherings, gift-giving, and rejoicing.

Bahä'i

Founded

The Bahä'i Faith began in 1844.

Founder

The Bahä'i Faith was founded in Persia (Iran) by Mirza Husayn Ali Nuri (1817-1892) known as Bahäulläh, the "Glory of God." The word Bahä'i is derived from Bähe ("glory" or "splendor") and means follower of Bahäulläh.

The Bahä'i Faith began in 1844 in Shiraz, Persia (now Iran), when a young merchant named Sayyid Ali Muhammad, also known as the Bäb (the Gate of God), proclaimed himself to be the Promised One of Islam, the Qaim, and said that the mission of his dispensation was to alert the people that another prophet would soon come to unite the world and bring universal peace to all. The Bäb was executed in 1850 at the age of 31. Over 20,000 followers of the Bäb died as martyrs for his cause.

In 1863, Bahäulläh announced that he was the messenger foretold by the Bäb, sent by God to establish a universal faith. He endured a series of exiles and imprisonments and finally was banished to the prison city of Acre, Palestine. He died in 1892 while still under house arrest.

Major Scriptures

The Bahä'i writings include numerous works by Bahäulläh, the Prophet-Founder, and interpretations by his son, 'Abdul-Bahä, and great-grandson, Shoghi Effendi. Bahä'i literature can be read today in over 750 languages and dialects.

The writings of Bahäulläh include 100 volumes of Arabic and Persian text in many literary styles, which is considered to be revelation from God. Some of the major texts include:

- Kitab-i-Aqdas (The Most Holy Book): which describes the details of a new World Order
- Kitab-i-Iqan (The Book of Certitude): which describes the doctrinal writings
- The Hidden Words: which describes the ethical teachings
- The Seven Valleys: poetic and mystical writings

The writings of Abdul Bahä and Shoghi Effendi (who translated most of the Bahä'i scripture into English) also have special significance.

In addition, Bahä'is acknowledge the sacredness of and make use of the scriptures of the world's other religions.

Sects

There are no formal sects within Bahä'i.

Adherents

The Bahä'i world community includes almost all nationalities, classes, trades and professions. There are over 5 million Bahä'is living in many countries around the world.

Goals

The central principles of the Bahä'i Faith are the oneness of God, the oneness of Religion, and the oneness of Mankind. Bahä'is believe that humanity is one family created by God.

The purpose of human life is to know and to worship God and to carry forward an ever advancing civilization. The Bahä'is strive to bring about the unity of mankind, world peace, and world order.

Path of Attainment

The fostering of good character and the development of spiritual qualities such as honesty, trustworthiness, compassion, and justice is the primary path of the faith.

Prayer, meditation, and work done in the spirit of service to humanity are important Bahä'i disciplines.

Bahä'is are obligated to practice chastity and monogamy; marriage requires consent of both parties and their parents.

Use of alcohol and drugs is prohibited except when prescribed by a physician.

The eradication of prejudice of race, creed, class, nationality, and sex is the primary motto of the faith.

Bahä'is observe a fast between sunrise and sundown during the last month of their calendar (March 2 - 20).

Synopsis

The Bahä'i Faith is an independent world religion with adherents in virtually every country.

The Prophet Bahäulläh taught that divine Revelation is a Continuous and Progressive process and that the mission of the Messengers of God represent successive stages in the spiritual evolution of human society.

Bahäulläh's eldest son, Abbäs Effendi (1844 – 1921) known as Abdul Bahä (Servant of Bahä), led the community as the perfect exemplar and infallible interpreter of his teachings.

Abdul Bahä's grandson, Shoghi Effendi Rabbäni (1896 – 1957), was appointed to be the Guardian of the Bahä Faith. He established the Bahä'i administrative order and supervised the spread of the Faith to all parts of the globe.

The international governing body is called the Universal House of Justice which is the supreme administrative body of the Bahä'i Faith following the death of Shoghi Effendi. Its members are elected once every five years in Haifa, Israel at an international convention. All Bahä'i elections are by secret ballot, with no nominations or electioneering.

The Bahä'i Administrative Order is free from any form of ecclesiasticism, having neither priesthood nor man-made rituals, and forbids asceticism, monasticism, and mendicancy. The clearly defined administration has protected the unity of the Bahä Faith from schism.

There are currently over 25,000 local assemblies and over 145 National Assemblies throughout the world.

The affairs of the local Bahä'i community are administered by a Spiritual Assembly consisting of nine-members elected annually. Nationally, a nine-member body is elected each year by the delegates of local assemblies.

Bahä'i meetings include devotional services, readings from Bahä'i and other religious scriptures, study classes, discussions, social events, and the observance of holy days.

Bahä'is do not enroll in political parties, but are encouraged to vote and be active in community affairs.

The eradication of prejudice of race, creed, class, nationality, and sex is the primary motto of the faith. Racism retards the unfoldment of the boundless potentialities of its victims, corrupts its perpetrators, and blights human progress. Recognition of the oneness of mankind, implemented by appropriate legal measures, must be universally upheld if this problem is to be overcome.

Belief in the equality of women and men. The denial of such equality perpetrates an injustice against one half of the world's population and promotes harmful attitudes in men that are carried from the family to the workplace, to political life, and ultimately to international relations.

Baha'i World Center

The spiritual and administrative center of the Faith has been established in the Holy Land of Akka and Haifa. The Bahä'i holy places in Israel consist of the shrines of Bahäulläh and the Bäb and historic sites associated with them. The Universal House of Justice is located on Mt. Carmel in Haifa.

Houses of Worship (Baha'i Temple)

Throughout the world Bahä'is have built several Houses of Worship for prayer and meditation. Services of worship consist of the recitation of Bahä'i scriptures and scriptures of the other divinely revealed religions. Sometimes "a Capella" music is played.

Bahä'is believe the number nine symbolizes completeness and hence Bahä'i temples are designed with nine sides, with a door on each side. At present, seven Bahä'i temples exist in the following location: Wilmette (Chicago) Illinois, USA; Frankfurt-am-Main, West Germany; Kampala, Uganda; Sidney, Australia; Panama City, Panama; New

Delhi, India; and Apia, Western Samoa. Eventually, each locality will have its own house of worship, which will serve as the point around which the scientific, educational, humanitarian, and administrative institutions of the Bahä'i community revolve.

Social and Economic Development

Due to the progress of civilization, social laws change in the society at large. Hence from time to time each new revelation (religion) reflects such change to further enhance the spirituality of the people. Thus the principles of Bahä'i Faith calls for racial unity, elimination of all prejudice, promotion of gender equality, economic justice, universal compulsory education, global patriotism, and ecological sensitivity.

Bahä'i communities throughout the world are involved in social and economic development activities that serve the needs of local populations. The institutions and programs are mostly supported by voluntary contributions from members.

Activities in health and social services, communications, agriculture and forestry, and community development are done in the spirit of service to mankind. Social and economic development projects worldwide include medical centers, programs for women, cooperative savings programs, building renovations, communal farms and homes for refugees and for the aged. The majority of the projects is the result of grass root efforts operating with little or no outside support.

The Bahä'i Faith calls for the establishment of a universal auxiliary language to facilitate global communication, and a world federal system through which all nations may work for the good of the humanity.

Ignorance is indisputably the principal reason for the decline and fall of people and the perpetuation of prejudice. No nation can achieve success unless education is accorded in all its citizens. This belief has inspired the establishment of learning centers which include tutorial schools in fifteen African countries and more than 300 training schools and centers in Asia. Seven educational radio stations currently operate in Liberia, Panama, Chile, Peru, Bolivia, Ecuador and the United States to serve the local population. Programs in native languages offer advice on health care, crop management, and child development.

United Nations Activity

The Bahä'i International Community is affiliated with the United Nations Economic and Social Council (ECOSOC), with the United Nations Children's Fund (UNICEF), and with the United Nations Environment Program (UNEP). Local Bahä'i communities are encouraged to support UN's various humanitarian projects. The Bahä'i International Community participates in meetings of UN agencies concerned with human rights, social development, the status of women, the environment, human settlement, food, science and technology, population, the law of the sea, crime prevention, substance abuse, disarmament, and the United Nations University.

Beliefs

The Bahä'i Faith stresses unity. The central principles are the Oneness of God, the Oneness of Religion, and the Oneness of Mankind. God sent the prophets and key figures of all the world religions to further the continuing advancement of civilization. This means that all the world's great religions are successive stages in God's revelation. Bahä'i faith provides the divine guidance necessary for this Age.

Believe in the equality of men and women. All humans have a common origin and hence all people deserve to be treated equally. Baha'i's purpose is to foster love, unity, and peace.

The sacred writings of all world religions teach the same spiritual truth. Hence it encourages interreligious dialogue and marriage across racial, ethnic, or religious lines. Thus its membership represents every culture and ethnic group promoting unity while preserving cultural diversity.

Bahä'i principles include the essential harmony of science and religion and independent investigation of truth.

Bahä'i believe the number nine has special significance. It is the highest single digit, which symbolizes completeness. Bahä'is have faith in the covenant made by Bahäulläh that a Promised One will appear after one thousand years.

Symbol

Three horizontal lines represent God, His Messengers, and humanity. The vertical line represents the Message linking all three.

Two stars represent God's Twin Messengers; the Bäb and Bahäulläh.

Holidays

The Bahä'i Faith began in 1844. The Bahä'i calendar divides the year into nineteen months of nineteen days each. Four days (five in the leap year) are added between the eighteenth and nineteenth months to keep it synchronized with the solar calendar.

The Bahä'i year includes nine holy days and a period of fasting near the end of the year. On holidays, work is suspended and a celebration includes family time, worship, and festive foods.

- The Ridvän Festival - commemorates Bahäulläh's proclamation that he is the Messenger of God for this day - an event which took place in Baghdad's Garden of Ridvän (Persian for paradise) - (April 21 - May 2, with abstention from work or school on April 21, April 29, and May 2)

- Declaration of the Bäb - celebrates the event with which the Bahä'i faith marks its beginning (May 23)

- Ascension of Bahäulläh - the anniversary of Bahäulläh's passing (May 29)

- Martyrdom of the Bäb - marks the Bäb's execution (July 9)

- Birth of the Bäb (October 20)

- Birth of Bahäulläh (November 12)

- Naw Ruz (Persian for "New Day") - celebrates the end of the Bahä'i nineteen day fast and the beginning of the Bahä'i New Year (March 21)

Other annual Bahä'i observances do not require abstinence from work or school.

Naked Child

On the street I saw a naked child, hungry and shivering in the cold. I became angry and said to God, "Why do you allow this? Why don't you do something?"

God did not reply. That night he said, quite suddenly, "I certainly did something. I made you."

Comparison:
Indian and Western Religions

Indian (I) and Western (W) Religions

Creation of the Universe

(I):   The universe exists in endless cycles of creation, preservation, and destruction. There is no absolute end to the universe. Universe is eternal. There is no duality of God and universe but a unity (God is Universe and Universe is God). Hence every living being and object of the universe is a part of God.

(W):   The world was created by God at some point in time. In the future it will be forever destroyed by Him. God is separate from the universe and rules it from above. It stresses a dualistic nature of the world.

The True God

(I):   There is but one true and absolute God or Self. All souls are destined to receive Liberation or God's grace through experience on many paths according to their understanding, temperament, and maturity. God is pure love and consciousness.

(W):   There is but one true God and one true religion. Those who accept it will enjoy God's grace. All others, unless they repent and come to God, will suffer eternally in Hell. God is loving as well as wrathful.

Proof of God

(I):   Proof of God's existence and His compassion towards all living being exists in the self realization of an individual, which in turn directly communicates with God / Self. The indirect proof is through the enlightened Guru (teacher) and the revealed scriptures.

(W):   Proof of God's existence and His love and promise for man is in the Prophets and in His unchanging and unique scriptures revealed through the Prophets.

Knowing of God

(I): Personal, inner and often mystical experience of God / Self is the crux of religion. Man can and ultimately must realize God / Self during earthly life. Knowledge of God / Self is individually oriented and introspective.

(W): It is essential for man to seek personal knowledge of God. The linchpin of religion is not experience but belief and faith, coupled with a virtuous life. It is socially oriented and extroverted.

Man's Plight

(I): Man's suffering is due to ignorance of his self. He is forever on a progressive spiritual path which leads from ignorance to knowledge, from death to immortality.

(W): Man's suffering is due to disobedience to God's will, to non-belief and non-accepting of His law.

Hell

(I): God is Compassionate and is inextricably one with the soul, guiding it through karma into religion (Dharma) and finally to liberation. Hell is a lower astral realm, it is not eternal. It exists as a period of Karmic suffering.

(W): On Judgment Day the physical body of every soul that ever lived is brought to life. God consigns virtuous (pure) souls to heaven and sinners to Hell. Hell is a physical place where the body burns without being consumed and one suffers the anguish of knowing that he will never be with God.

Evil

(I): There is no intrinsic evil, all is good and all is God. No force in the world or in man opposes God, though the veiling instinctive intellectual mind keeps us from knowledge of Him.

(W): There is indeed genuine evil in the world, a living force which opposes God's will. This evil is embodied in Satan and partially in man as one of his tendencies.

Enlightenment and Salvation

(I): The goals of enlightenment and liberation are to be found in this life, within the context of time and within man himself. Salvation is through self realization or strict obedience to God's will through one's knowledge or the descent of His grace through complete surrendering and selfless service. Beliefs may be dual or non-dual. Salvation is achieved here and now.

(W): Salvation comes at the end of the world, at the end of time, and has nothing to do with enlightenment. The belief is strictly dualistic. Salvation is achieved through strict obedience to God's will, usually through a messiah, prophet, or priest.

Destiny

(I): The purpose of life is to evolve, through experience, into higher spiritual destiny and ultimately to liberation. Acquiring the things of the world is not the purpose of life.

(W): Man's destiny lies beyond this world, which is but an opportunity for earning eternal joy or suffering.

Paths to God

(I): Man is free to choose his own path, for all paths lead ultimately to God / true Self. Sin is only of the mind, not of the soul, which is pure. There is no Judgment Day for God does not judge or punish.

(W): Only one path leads to God, all others are false and futile. Everyone must accept the one true religion. If this is not done, the soul, laden with sin, will be damned on Judgment Day.

Virtues

(I): Virtuous conduct and right belief are the foundation of religious life, the first step toward higher mystical communion. Moral living is essential to spiritual progress. Liberation requires knowledge and personal attainment, not mere belief. Unrighteous thoughts, words, and deeds keep one from liberation.

(W):   Religion is based on ethical and moral conduct, for the opposite leads one away from God. If one obeys God's commands for a moral and ethical life and believes in Him and in His Prophets such as Moses, Jesus, Mohammed, or Zoroaster, salvation is assured.

Religion Origin

(I):   Religion is cosmic, eternal, transcending human history, which is cyclical. Stress is placed on revelation of God's presence in the here and now.

(W):   Religion is historical, beginning with a prophet or event. Stress is on the past and on future rewards or punishments. History is linear, never to be repeated.

Reality

(I):   There is more to reality than what we experience with the five senses. The soul is immortal, deathless, eternal, and ultimately liberated from rebirth and misery.

(W):   There is more to reality than the things of this world. The soul is immortal, deathless, eternal, and living forever in God's presence in heaven or separated from Him in Hell.

Doctrine

(I):   Doctrines tend to be subtle, complex, and even paradoxical. Freedom to worship and to believe in a variety of ways is predominant. Other paths are accepted as God's divine will at work. It is universal and tolerant.

(W):   Doctrines tend to be simple, clear, and rational. Worship and belief are formalized, exacting, and required. Other paths are endured, but not honored. It is exclusionist and dogmatic.

Sainthood

(I):   The path to saintliness is through self discipline, purification, concentration and contemplation. Value is placed on ascetic ideals, individual religious practice (Sädhanä), yoga, and super conscious awakening.

(W):   Path to saintliness is through self sacrifice, submission to God and concern for others. Value is placed on good work, social concerns, and scriptural study, with little emphasis on yoga and meditation.

Worship

(I):   Worship is individual, highly ritualistic, and meditative. It centers around the temple and home shrine all days of the week.

(W):   Worship is congregational, simple in its rituals, centering around the church, synagogue, or mosque, mostly on a Sabbath day.

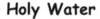

Holy Water

Tukaram the saintly poet of India once travelled on foot all the way from Maharashtra state to Banaras to bring holy water of the river Ganges for a Grand Bath ceremony (Abhisheka) of his deity (God).

On his way with the holy water in a copper pot, he saw a donkey lying almost dead on the ground, suffering from the scorching heat of the sun. Seeing the donkey suffering without water, his tender heart was moved with compassion. He spontaneously poured the precious holy water which was meant for the deity in the mouth of the donkey.

Soon after the donkey drank the water, he slowly came to life and opened his eyes. There was an expression of satisfaction on his face, the donkey was alive.

Tukaram seeing the donkey revived back to life took a great sigh of relief and experienced a spiritual ecstasy. He said to himself, "My Abhisheka to God is complete," and returned home without holy water.

References and Bibliography

A four page article, an insert of the Hinduism Today newspaper of April 1993 and its earlier version.

Parliament of World Religions 1993

A.K.Lad, The Concept of Liberation in Indian Philosophy (Burhanpur M.P. India), 1967)

Huston Smith, The Religions of Man (Harper & Row, 1965).

Geoffrey Parrinder, World Religions from Ancient History to the Present (Facts on File Publications, NY, 1984)

International Religious Foundation, World Scripture A Comparative Anthology of Sacred Texts (Paragon House NY, 1991)

Swami Shivananda Saraswati (Rushikesh), World's Religions (Gujarati book 1970)

Editorial Staff of Life, The World's Great Religions Vol. 1 to 3 (1963 edition)

Haridas Bhattacharya, The Cultural Heritage of India Vol IV (The Ramkrishana Mission, Calcutta, India 1956)

Antheony de Mello, S.J., The Song of the Bird - 1996

Academic American Encyclopedia

World Book of Encyclopedia

Internet Searches of Various Religions

U.S. Bahä'i Office of Public Information pamphlet

Long Island Interfaith Book

Watch Tower Bible, Mankind's Search for God (International Bible Student Association, NY)

Quotations

Man's natural spirituality is best expressed in loving and practical aid to his fellow man, rather than metaphysical inquiry.

Humanitarianism

All actions create their opposing forces, and the wise will seek inaction in action.

The Taote Ching

I forgive all living beings; let all living beings forgive me
I have friendship with all and enmity towards none

Jain creed

The place to be happy is 'here',
The time to be happy is 'present'
The way to be happy is 'to make others happy'.

- A wise man -

My stomach is not a graveyard for dead animals.

George Bernard Shaw

Moral and spiritual uprightness are the cornerstone of religious ethics and in the supreme value of loyalty to all your acts.

Shintoism

All problems of existence are essentially problems of harmony.

Sri Aurobindo

Human nature is inherently good, and evil is an unnatural condition arising from disharmony.

Confucianism

"We are as much alive as we keep the earth alive."

- Chief Dan George (Native Spirituality)

"We affirm and promote respect for the interdependent web of all existence of which we are a part."

- Unitarian principle

That there is no God beyond the Divine within man and no truth beyond existential freedom, that all organized religions imprison man, causing repression, fear and poverty.

Osho Rajneesh